W~~OMAN~~ASP

The Life, Career, and Murder of Hollywood's Susan Cabot

Lona Bailey

W~~OMAN~~ WASP

The Life, Career, and Murder of Hollywood's Susan Cabot

HISTRIA
A&E

Histria A&E

Las Vegas ◊ London ◊ New York ◊ Palm Beach

Published in the United States of America by
Histria Books
7181 N. Hualapai Way, Ste. 130-86
Las Vegas, NV 89166 USA
HistriaBooks.com

Histria A&E is an imprint of Histria Books dedicated to outstanding books that focus on arts and entertainment. Titles published under the imprints of Histria Books are distributed in the United States and Canada by Simon & Schuster and worldwide through Unified Book Distribution. We appreciate your support of copyright by purchasing an authorized edition of this book and for respecting intellectual property laws by not reproducing, scanning, or otherwise distributing any part of it by any means without permission. You are supporting authors and enabling Histria Books to continue publishing books for everyone.

All rights reserved. No part of this book may be reprinted or reproduced or utilized in any form or by any electronic, mechanical or other means, now known or hereafter invented, including photocopying and recording, or in any information storage or retrieval system, without the permission in writing from the Publisher. No part of this book may be used or reproduced in any manner for the purpose of training artificial intelligence technologies or systems.

Library of Congress Control Number: 2025944905

ISBN 978-1-59211-679-9 (softbound)
ISBN 978-1-59211-705-5 (eBook)

Copyright © 2026 by Lona Bailey

Contents

Author's Note 7

Chapter One — Harriet Pearl Shapiro — Orphan 11

Chapter Two — California's No Italy, But It'll Do 28

Chapter Three — B-Movie Mania 55

Chapter Four — Timothy Scott Roman: A Study in Statistics 72

Chapter Five — A Family at Last 90

Chapter Six — Drying Inward from the Edge 104

Chapter Seven — Ninjas & Blunt Force Trauma 119

Chapter Eight — The Trial of Susan Cabot Roman 133

Chapter Nine — Final Discussion and Call to Action 158

Appendix — Selected Screen Performances of Susan Cabot 178

Bibliography 184

Author's Note

As a popular B-list movie actress in the 1940s-1950s whose grisly slaying perhaps gained her more notoriety than her on-screen and on-stage accomplishments, Susan Cabot has a significant, but sordid legacy. There are piles of misinformation when it comes to various seasons of Susan's life, as well as the circumstances surrounding her death. Susan Cabot was a complex person with a complex history, making this biographic assembly a considerable undertaking.

With her dark hair and dark eyes, Susan Cabot was often cast in "exotic" roles of feminine minorities from her first credited film role in William Berke's *On the Isle of Samoa* (1950) until her last in John Barnwell's *Surrender-Hell!* (1959). She was featured across several genres but was especially lauded in Westerns such as Jesse

Hibbs' *Ride Clear of Diablo* (1954) with Audie Murphy, film noir such as Roger Corman's *Machine-Gun Kelly* (1958) with Charles Bronson, and a number of other Corman films, such as *Carnival Rock* (1957) with Brian G.

Hutton, *Sorority Girl* (1957) with Dick Miller, and most notably *The Wasp Woman* (1959) with Anthony Eisley (aka Fred Eisley). The role for which Susan was most recognized was "Janice Starlin," the president of a cosmetics corporation who experiments with a youth serum made from the extract of wasps that proves to have deadly side effects, not unlike the experimental injections that contributed to her own real-life slaughter in 1986 at the hands of her son, who suffered from dwarfism.

One of the most compelling elements of Susan's story is how her on-screen roles increasingly bled over into her tragic reality to such a profound extent that many see her own slaying as a reflection of her *Wasp Woman* performance. Susan's only child, Timothy, was born prematurely with a number of lifelong health issues, one of which was dwarfism. There are eerie parallels between Susan's personal life and film work, most poignantly in Corman's *The Wasp Woman* (1959). The sci-fi themes in the classic cult film seemed to play out in Susan's life *and* death, with experimental injections leading to murder both on-screen and off.

The end of Susan's life was reportedly a bit reminiscent of *Grey Gardens*, *Whatever Happened to Baby Jane?*, and *Sunset Boulevard* all rolled into one, though what led to the diabolical manifestation of that trichotomy isn't quite as eerie as perhaps we would like it to be. Susan Cabot was a beautiful, intelligent, capable actress who exercised an immense amount of personal grit in overcoming an impoverished childhood, personal challenges in romance and motherhood, and scaling Hollywood's "Studio System" in the 1940s and 1950s. This book is the first to comprehensively tell the tale of Susan Cabot's bizarre legacy of moxie, madness, and murder. Much has been publicized about her son Tim's victimization leading to her murder, but with this fresh interpretation of her life and death through her son's murder trial court records, Susan's side of the story is finally told. Was Susan Cabot the vain, venomous monster who turned her son into a science project like the papers said? Or was she in fact a loving, devoted mother who suddenly became the victim of a deranged man-child who had himself gone mad? Or does the truth lie somewhere in between these two extremes?

Despite Susan Cabot's legacy of triumph and tragedy, she merely has a sectional mention in three print anthologies among other "B-list actors and actresses," but prior to this book, she has no full-length biographic work dedicated to her contribution to entertainment and her rather convoluted personal life and brutal death. While Susan was admittedly not an A-lister luminary, she became a beautiful, tragic archetype for how reality can be eerily influenced by fantasy.

In Susan's most memorable film, *The Wasp Woman* (1959), her character "Janice" is given "experimental injections" that transform her into the deadly creature who kills several innocent people before being destroyed herself. In an attempt to "treat" Tim's dwarfism, Susan gave him experimental injections (prescribed by his physician) for most of his life, which resulted in many physical and psychological complications, including aggressive tendencies. When Susan was 59 and Tim 22, he bludgeoned her to death with a weightlifting bar in their LA mansion. Police found her bedroom a bloodbath with linens over what was left of her face. "I think Roman is just a statistic that went bad," Deputy District Attorney Bradford

E. Stone said during Tim's first jury trial. Though Tim was arrested, it was Susan who was tried and convicted of her own murder in allegedly driving her son to the point of matricide. Susan's side of the story has never been told until now.

This biography was written in the spirit of the Latin word *redemptio*, meaning "redemption" or "to buy back." My hope was to "buy back" the legacy of Susan Cabot in a more balanced retelling of her story outside the misogynistic media circus and courtroom proceedings of her brutal murder. I have tried, through this book, to carefully sand off the inaccurate layers of oil paint that lawyers, doctors, judges, and news reporters so sloppily painted over the self-portrait Susan had spent fifty-nine years painting. The two main colors used by the misogynistically framed court proceedings and media circus were the thick matte swamp green of victim-blaming and the glossy candy apple red of mother-blaming. In sharing her story from a more balanced and feminist perspective, those imposed layers have been sanded off, and by the end of the book, I hope readers will clearly see the beautiful, radiant self-portrait Susan Cabot painted over the course of her lifetime.

One of the most compelling reasons to share the true self-portrait of Susan Cabot *now* is best answered through one of my favorite Dr. Martin Luther King, Jr. quotes: "Injustice anywhere is a threat to justice everywhere. We are caught in an inescapable network of mutuality, tied in a single garment of destiny. Whatever affects one directly affects all indirectly." Justice never goes out of style, so thirty-seven years after Susan's death, it's surely time to set the record straight.

Like any compelling Hollywood story, there are conflicting accounts and waves of controversy surrounding Susan Cabot's life, death, and legacy. My bedrock hope for this book is that a more balanced understanding of her life, death, and legacy can be established in the wake of the current imbalance, which favors a more negative perspective. In short, this is an effort in redemptive framing based on a fresh approach to a figure long misunderstood.

Given the passage of time, the loss or sealing of key records, and the conflicting accounts that survive, the life and death of Susan Cabot remain complex and open to interpretation. As the researcher and author of this book, I claim no ultimate authority on Susan Cabot's life, death, and enduring legacy. In creating a more comprehensive account of Susan in this book, I have pulled from available sources and presented the piecemeal "facts" in narrative format. If readers walk away from this book with more questions than answers about Susan Cabot's life—good, as I, her biographer have done the same, after researching and writing about her. I do, however, believe she was unfairly "convicted" of her own murder, and that is something that is just as unjust today as it was thirty-seven years ago.

So, in defense of artist, actress, and devoted mother, Susan Cabot Roman, I am sincerely,

Dr. Lona Bailey

Chapter One
Harriet Pearl Shapiro — Orphan

"The truth is you can be orphaned again and again and again...and the secret is, this will hurt less and less each time until you can't feel a thing."

— Chuck Palahniuk

"911, what is your emergency?" asked the dispatcher on the other end of the phone. "My mother. She's dead," Timothy Roman calmly stated. Several hours later, B-movie queen, Susan Cabot, was found by responders in her Encino mansion master bedroom. Her headless body was in eerily good condition, lying flat in a purple negligée. If it weren't for the bloodbath found inside the room, she would have looked as if she were just peacefully sleeping—from the neck down.

***

Susan Cabot was born "Harriet Pearl Shapiro" on July 9, 1927, at St. Elizabeth's Hospital in Brighton, Massachusetts, about five miles from her Boston home. Her parents, Philip and Muriel (Shortes) Shapiro, were of stout Russian-Jewish heritage; both were born in Russia and migrated with their respective families to America's Northeast in the early 1910s. The two met in their small Jewish community in Chelsea, Massachusetts, and after a traditional courtship, married on March 9, 1924. Philip was twenty-three, and Muriel was twenty-one.

The two made their newlywed settlement in Dorchester where Philip, who had worked as a grocer in Chelsea since his early teens, took a position as a hardware salesman. Muriel worked as a part-time bookkeeper and tended their rented one-bedroom in the newly built apartment house on Johnston Rd. The Shapiros of Dorchester seemed to have a bright start in eclipsing their own cramped childhoods of scarcity…at first.

Philip and Muriel were both hard workers, and like their families of origin, zealous in their Jewish faith. They were active in the Temple Ohabei Shalom, then located on Union Park Street in Chelsea. Muriel was beautiful, with dark hair and eyes, and had quite an elaborate skincare routine passed down from her mother, Tillie, that involved weekly egg yolk facials. Though dutiful in her bookkeeping position, housework, and physical appearance, she was also prone to sways of emotional faintness, which irritated Philip's pragmatism. The two were known to have frequent (and loud) disputes in their Johnston Rd. one-bedroom. With the feather-thin walls of their apartment house, other tenants heard the angry crescendos of Yiddish clearly and often.

In 1926, Muriel became pregnant with their first child and on July 9, 1927, gave birth to Harriet Pearl Shapiro. Muriel quit her bookkeeping position to care for the wispy, black-haired baby girl who didn't seem to grow even an inch her entire first year of life. Philip and Muriel both were of petite proportions, and Harriet Pearl was no different.

Boston's Dorchester

Boston was founded in 1630 as the central hub of Puritan colonization in the separatists' New England establishment. Because of the unique topography of what was originally called "Shawmut Peninsula," Massachusetts' capital city is fixated on Massachusetts Bay, which helped initially establish it as a prosperous commercial seaport in the 1700s.

Boston has been a central figure in American history since its founding, with some of the most legendary events in the nation having marched right through its Market Square. American colonizers regarded the city as the commonwealth's epicenter during the American Revolution that saw the Boston Massacre, the Boston Tea Party, and Paul Revere's infamous midnight ride.

Railroad systems in the American Northeast were constructed in the mid-1800s, and Boston had its own innovative system of tracks by 1842, along with its own steamship line in the estuary of Boston Harbor. During the blaze of the Civil War from 1861 to 1865, Boston served as a Union base with a strong abolitionist presence. Boston financially mobilized Massachusetts state troops to fight in favor of reunification under abolitionist policies.

During the Reconstruction Era, subways and streetcars moved into Boston's downtown district, which served to bolster manufacturing efforts in the city's industrialization throughout the late 1800s and early 1900s.

Boston may be considered a "small town," according to its size and traditions, but it has long been a progressive political, educational, and socio-economic giant in its culture and accomplishments. As the seat of Suffolk County, the city has been home to some of the most legendary writers, inventors, social reformers, and political figures of American history. Among many others, Boston gave our world the genius of John F. Kennedy, Clara Barton, Alexander Graham Bell, Edgar Allan Poe, Robert Frost, and Harvard University.

The six-square-mile area of Dorchester was originally its own city built over the Neponset River. Boston officially established it as a Bostonian district in 1870. The turn of the twentieth century's industry boom brought a vast influx of immigrant workers of diverse heritages into the metropolitan area that Boston was becoming. Much of that population settled in Dorchester, and the once "little village" began developing into "Boston's streetcar suburb" with a melting pot population of Irish, German, Latino, Italian, and Russian inhabitants. Along with the laying of streetcar lines and the establishment of manufacturing plants came three-story apartment buildings, referred to as "tightly packed triple-deckers," constructed to house the vast influx of workers and their families.

In 1920, Boston's population had grown to well over 740,000, with many of that number residing in its developing urban areas. For its 48.4

square mile region, the city was electric with industry, diversity, and oppidan congestion, especially for the migrant working class of which the Shapiros were a part.

Philip and Muriel were active in the Jewish immigrant community of Dorchester and lived and worked in a loud, lively hub of working middle class. Their days and nights folded over on each other in blurs of Muriel's faded print dresses and smoky nights of Philip and his poker buddies around their kitchen table. The melding of Philip's hard-nosed pragmatism and Muriel's emotional fragility in the vacuum of working-class volatility proved unsustainable. Their individual approaches to their oppressive reality more than burdened the other and the ears of their triple-decker neighbors through feather-thin walls.

The Yellow Wallpaper

After Harriet's birth, Muriel's mental state deteriorated. Her lifelong depressive proclivities were stirred to manic undulations with the dance of undiagnosed postpartum depression. In an era that had little understanding of the condition and its ramifications, there were no resources or support systems for Muriel in her suffering. Philip was sympathetic toward Muriel's state, to a point, but having no context for such things, he began to shut her out more and more with each escalating "episode."

It is unknown how long Muriel's postpartum depression—and eventual psychosis—lasted, but long enough to cause serious upset for the entire household. She and Philip had dug their way into a patterned hole of fighting from which neither could climb out. Charlotte Perkins Gilman's 1892 groundbreaking short story *The Yellow Wallpaper* was becoming the Shapiros' untoward reality.

In the feminist classic, Gilman's narrator spirals into insanity within the symbolism of the deteriorating "yellow wallpaper" of her rented room. Muriel was one of the millions of reflections of Gilman's frightful tale of the female plight after childbirth, for she too could have echoed Gilman's words: "I cry at nothing, and cry most of the time… Nobody would believe what an effort it is to do what little I am able, - to dress and entertain, and order things."

Despite Muriel's condition that seemed only to deteriorate as the months passed, there were fleeting happy moments for Harriet, though most were experienced outside of their one-bedroom in the Johnston Rd. triple-decker. Muriel was just as particular about little Harriet's appearance as she had been about her own, often dressing her in "store-bought" cotton frocks and almost fanatically arranging her toddler curls. On a rare holiday, the family of three (plus Harriet's favorite Teddy Bear) day tripped to Boston Harbor Beach, where she fell in love with its picturesque view and the temporary spell of calm it seemed to cast over her usually feuding parents. Though the trips were infrequent, they became some of the most treasured of Harriet's whole life.

By her first year in primary school, Harriet was more than accustomed to her parents' almost nightly brawls and the hollow winces of their aftermath. After what seemed like hours of their quarreling, stonewalling, and quarreling again pattern, Philip would often blaze out the door with that familiar, sharp slam behind him echoed by Muriel's wails. Harriet was always left alone to tend to her mother's frailty in the fallout of her parents' contention.

Harriet had been given a lonely, confusing charge at the young ages of four and five in emotionally caregiving for her mother.

One particular night, when Philip stormed down the steps of their Johnston Rd. triple-decker, he made good on his years of threats, and didn't come back. When his usual, chilly return the next morning or next evening didn't come, Muriel began to panic. For days, Muriel vacillated between hysterics and catatonia, wondering when and if he would come home. She was angry, then panicked, then angry again, fearing Philip had been hurt, killed, or had finally gone through with his frequent threats of desertion.

In her grievous abandonment, something in Muriel's psyche resigned. Almost forgetting she had a child, she let everything around her mount in squalor while Harriet was left to care for herself. The Shapiro apartment was eerily quiet through its feather-thin walls as neighboring tenants noticed little Harriet coming and going on her own for several days. After the landlady paid their room a collection visit for overdue rent, she phoned the state office. Authorities found Muriel, in her dejected state, unfit to care for Harriet, and both Shapiro women were taken into state custody. Muriel was taken to Gardner State Hospital about sixty miles outside of Boston, while Harriet was state-stamped "orphan."

Muriel had two sisters who also lived close to the Shapiros' Johnston Rd. home, but neither were interested in taking Harriet to raise. Philip made good on his threats of leaving Muriel and Harriet that time; he moved to Connecticut and never looked back. He eventually remarried and started a new family and career while the state took over the identities of Muriel and Harriet. Muriel was barred with only "yellow wallpaper" to occupy her, while Harriet fell into the brutal cogs of Massachusetts' foster care.

Foster Care

The foster care model goes back to biblical times, as does its convoluted reputation. In America's early 1900s, however, independent social agencies began forming in metropolitan areas to place orphaned or abused children with vetted families in part to "clean up the streets" that saw a growing population of displaced children.

Eventually, the government obtained control over those agencies thereby establishing the scaffolding of what we know today as the federal child welfare system.

In the 1930s, foster care wasn't far removed from its "orphan train" days in which displaced children were packed together in train cars and ferried across America's farmlands to be placed with surrogate families, many of whom just happened to need more hands for their rural spreads. The orphan train, established by independent philanthropic entities and the early aid efforts of social reformer Charles Loring Brace, was essentially a rolling orphanage scouting for placement homes for children found wandering urban streets or sleeping on piles of refuse in back alleys. Those placements of gloried emancipation from gutter life, however, were often just as bad or worse than the gutters themselves. The orphan trains often unknowingly delivered their trusting little riders to homesteads that saw them as nothing more than slaves. The movement lasted from 1854 to 1929 when child welfare laws changed, and of course the Great Depression struck down loads of social reform efforts due to lack of funds and staff. During the seventy-five years the orphan trains ran, more than 250,000 children rode the rails in search of "home."

Much like foster care itself, the orphan train movement has a similarly sordid legacy, as this philanthropic effort to aid children in dire circumstances often went awry due to insidious intentions of certain parties of authority and the insurmountable nature of it all with limited resources in such an era. Compared to the orphan train and institutionalization, however, foster care placements (which were often local) were an innovative idea. Regional foster care placement seemed more manageable for government agencies compared to the traditional brick-and-mortar orphanages that came with their own hosts of issues, and fleets of iron horses carting children around the country like freight. In the Northeast in the 1930s, local family placements for local children in state custody became the preferable governmental strategy. Children like Harriet were, theoretically, able to find "home" often within the cities in which they were born, which, like most things, came with both advantages and disadvantages.

Classic literature has long since glorified the orphan experience with Charles Dickens' "Oliver Twist," J.M. Barrie's "Peter Pan," and Mark Twain's "Tom Sawyer" among the most recognized. More contemporary media are replete with similar examples of orphans who champion beyond their difficult beginnings and find some corner of nobility as a result.

Media's lovable paladins in more recent years such as "Matilda" and "Harry Potter" who eventually rise above all their family of origin dejection are relatable, resilient icons whose survivalist plights have drawn sympathies from audiences for decades. The realities of an orphaned child's plight, however, especially in the 1930s, weren't as splendor-laden as classic or contemporary creatives suggest. Harriet was just one of the millions who privately labored on in loneliness bearing no magic, no heroism, and no shining triumph that righted all the wrongs of feeling unloved.

Harriet was old enough to remember the routine and "comfort" of home (however dysfunctional it might have been presented to her) along with both biological parents before the Shapiro family's dramatic rupture. Being physically taken from her home must have felt, in a way, like a kidnapping to someone so young. She surely watched in infernal horror as her mother was taken in one direction by authorities and she in the opposite. Neither knew exactly where they were being taken or if they would ever see each other again.

Beginning from roughly age six, Harriet was shuffled in and out of countless foster homes throughout Massachusetts, though she eventually was placed with a family in The Bronx, New York where she claimed to have done most of her growing up. She suffered myriad cruelties at the hands of both foster care workers and families with which she was placed—namely by the "father figures." From six to seventeen, Harriet was shuffled from home to home with only tattered fragments of an identity; she rarely felt she was more than a one-dimensional portrait of a poverty-stricken orphan nobody really wanted. Her transient existence gave way to what was later diagnosed by her psychologist, Dr. Carl Faber, as post-traumatic stress disorder after so many early developmental years of emotional, physical, and sexual abuse. Harriet once said she had always longed to be an artist, but due to her complex childhood, which she never publicly elaborated on, she had been "sidetracked." Author Laura Wagner opined that, "'sidetracked' was an understatement: It was more like a detour through Hell" for Harriet.

It isn't clear how long Harriet's birth mother, Muriel, was institutionalized, but by 1939, she had been discharged and shared an apartment with her mother, Tillie, in Brooklyn. Muriel began working in bookkeeping again after her stay at Gardner State. Though she may have tried to locate

Harriet after her discharge, because of the primitive nature of the foster care system at that time, it may have been next to impossible.

Muriel and Harriet didn't reconnect until years later, but during most of Harriet's teenage years, in and out of New York borough foster homes, she was only about forty miles from her mother's new life, whether she realized it or not.

Never Home

Most of Harriet's so-called "homes" were within tenement housing, a term which lends itself to a picture of provincial 1930s and 1940s "New York slums." The skinny, low-rise apartments or "tenement buildings" were erected in block systems in part to accommodate the immigration wave of the late 1800s. These structures were uniformly designed with compact quarters and back alleys separating units. They were initially built without electricity or plumbing, though eventually New York state housing authorities modified tenement amenities and included windows and fire escapes for each apartment.

Tenements in The Bronx were not altogether unlike Boston's "triple-deckers" where Harriet spent her first few years of life. In 1940, there were nearly 400,000 housing units in The Bronx, and because of the borough's population of 1.4 million, it wasn't uncommon for multigenerational families of six or seven to live in a cramped 300sq ft. apartment. For many tenement dwellers, home felt like a bricked box with no room for fresh air, individuality, or at times, even dignity. Though public housing was introduced to New York City in 1936, thereby doing away with the traditional "tenement" dwelling, remnants of those ill-famed structures and their cultural implications lasted far beyond 1936.

Most sources say Harriet lived in at least eight different foster homes (though one source says fourteen) between the ages of six and seventeen. The conditions of those homes were plausibly as bad as bad could get. Not only was Harriet, almost in an instant, thrust from lower middle class to abject poverty, but also from the Shapiros' small Dorchester nest she was thrown into an industrial metropolis with its relentless noise, smog, and shoulder-to-shoulder urbanite strangers.

She *and* her transient homes were unkempt with meager (or at times completely absent) basic necessities. Food and clean water were as scarce as privacy, with seemingly endless apartment units bunched in dirty bricked boxes.

The New York winters were too cold without enough heat, and the summers were too stuffy without enough ventilation in Harriet's lean-to tenement residences. At best, she was lonely with these temporary families that weren't truly hers, and at worst, scared for her very life.

Her teen years were blurs of back-alley clotheslines, often cold, meager rations called meals, and eternal chimney soot.

Unfortunately, some families during and immediately following the Great Depression saw the novelty of foster care as a way to make a quick buck at the expense of the child or children they were assigned. Much like today, foster families were often given a stipend by the state to help provide for the needs of the children in their custody. Some abused this system, and foster children were nearly worse off in-home than they had been before. When Harriet most needed love and parental tending, she found only bruises and perpetual shame.

Lost in the dungeoned cycle of constant transition, Harriet made one disastrous move after another. With every move, she, in a sense, felt orphaned over and over again. This cycle was often facilitated by the same traumatic narrative: Harriet would settle into a new placement with the embers of hope that just maybe this one would "be different." Those embers, however, quickly turned to cold ash with the realization that, once again, she was seen only as an indentured servant and/or a sexual conquest for her latest foster father figure. She was often awakened in the middle of the night by a large, slinking figure by her bed with devilish intentions she had no way of resisting. The stinging familiarity of those nights and clefted secrecy of the following days slowly drained Harriet of any remnants of self-dignity or personalistic wholeness. Sometimes she was removed from these homes for her safety, other times she was "given back" to the state for "another try."

Regarding her early days in that dichotomous cage of abuse and neglect, Harriet's decades-long psychologist, Dr. Carl Faber, said on the stand in her murder trial: "She had extreme irrational terror, as abused children and war veterans do, about these experiences, and was in and out of psychotherapy her whole adult life."

One of the most fragmenting aspects of Harriet's early years in and out of many different families was how her identity was forced to conform to whatever reality she was housed within at the time. Harriet was immersed in myriad religious, political, and ethnic worldviews during her years in foster care. While she later embraced elements of the "well-roundedness" that came from such exposure, as a child, the constant change was confusing and dehumanizing for her.

She was often covertly expected to deny her family's ethnoreligious Jewish heritage and adopt whatever religious preferences her hosting foster families had. As a child, she pledged allegiance at various points to both Protestantism and Catholicism due to the corresponding beliefs of her host families. Harriet was only able to tease out her own personally held beliefs once she reached middle age and had run the gamut of spiritual enlightenment from Buddhism to Atheism. The years between were full of existential qualms of the mystical that left her torn between her family of origin's Judaism and the smorgasbord of religious dogmas presented to her by her substitute families.

While residing with a middle-class Catholic family in The Bronx, teenage Harriet became intrigued by the Catholic doctrine and its ritualistic set of practices. It was all a little overwhelming to Harriet as she sat in Mass each week, but since she heard Psalm 27:10, she listened a bit closer to the homilies: "Though my father and mother forsake me, the LORD will receive me."

Among the most curious elements of Mass to her was the stoic, minimalistic presence of the nuns. The sisters and what they stood for seemed odd to young Harriet, but also a curious salve. The vows of chastity, poverty, and obedience taken by the Catholic nuns theoretically appealed to Susan in part because of the safety, predictability, and structure the Church would provide under those agreed-upon terms and conditions. Compared to the rat-infested, sexually violent homes she was surviving within, the clear, clean, minimalist picture of the sisters was incredibly appealing. They represented a sturdy lifeline in her gray spiral of constant change and constant victimization. Besides, nuns have always been known for their compassion toward orphans, and compassion was something Harriet had been deprived of for years. She studied these beacons from afar for weeks, and through study of Scripture and prayer, she finally got up the nerve to pledge her own allegiance to the Church.

She approached one of the sisters after Mass and blurted out her intent to become a nun. The sister was apparently caught off guard by the young girl's sudden and impassioned interest in a convent-lifestyle, and coolly asked *why* she wanted to become a nun. Harriet only had stutters for an answer, and the nun patronizingly shooed her on with a simple: "I don't believe this is for you."

That encounter with an ecumenical agent of God deeply affected Harriet. It felt like yet another rejection and an echo of the message everyone seemed to have for her of "sorry, we have no place for you here," which was the antithesis of Psalm 27:10.

Marty

Harriet was shuffled through her adolescence both home by home and school by school from Boston to Manhattan to Queens and finally The Bronx. She never stayed anywhere long enough to put down true roots, so close friends were scarce except for Marty. Martin "Marty" Sacker was the only semi-constant through her New York moves. There are conflicting accounts of how they initially came to know each other, but a best deduction is they were either schoolmates (despite their age difference) and/or neighborhood friends.

Much like Harriet, Marty was also of a Jewish immigrant family. The Sackers migrated from Poland to The Bronx before Marty was born in 1923. Aaron Sacker, Marty's father, worked as a blocker in millinery on the outskirts of Clinton Street's infamous "Millinery Row."

Though Marty was four years older than Harriet, he was one of the only stable figures in her life perhaps *ever*. He and his family had lived in the same apartment for years with little change to routine or dynamics. What the Sackers found to be ordinary drudgery, Harriet found to be a shining refuge.

The last two of Harriet's home placements in New York lasted longer than any had before, so she was able to engage more regularly with school in the same location for more than just a few months. In high school, she became interested in the fine arts of drawing, painting, sculpting, music, and dramatics. She became involved in theatre and found her vocal genius in elective musical studies. Fine arts and the humanities became the means by which she began rising above the anguish of her formative years.

Much like today, foster children generally remained in state custody and assigned home placement(s) until age eighteen. In some parts of the country during the 1930s and 1940s, a child did not reach his or her legal adulthood until age twenty-one. For many in the foster care system, their placements felt more like indentured servitude than a forever home. Whether Harriet merely had a few more months before her sentence within the cogs of the foster care system would end, or a few more years until she made it to twenty-one, she had had enough of back-alley everything.

Just a few weeks after her seventeenth birthday, as a means of escape more than passion, Harriet married twenty-one-year-old Marty Sacker on July 30, 1944, in Washington, D.C. When Harriet took "Sacker" as her new last name, she also took "Susan" as her new first.

By 1944, Marty was working full-time hours in dual careers: interior designer by day, painter by night. Marty lived and breathed the bohemian scene of Greenwich Village, and introduced Susan to the cabaret culture of the 1940s, which offered copious expressionistic opportunities for her own artistic skills.

Greenwich Village

Located in the heart of Manhattan, Greenwich Village has been a neighborhood steeped in history and cultural significance since its sixteenth-century origins. Dutch colonists tended the once Native American marshlands of Manhattan and in 1712 settled the village of "Grin'wich." The still rural Dutch colony was characterized by its rich farmland and sprawling colonial estates and became an agricultural oasis of the Northeast. Later in the nineteenth century's Gilded Age, the little farming village began developing into a bustling urban epicenter—making it an oasis of a different kind.

In the early 20th century, Greenwich Village became synonymous with artistic expression and sociopolitical liberation. The little Dutch colony had, by 1900, become known as a multicultural enclave simply called "The Village." Artists like Jackson Pollock, Mark Rothko, and Willem de Kooning found The Village to be soul-inspiring in their artistry. The neighborhood also played a pivotal role in the Beat Generation movement of the 1950s. Writers such as Jack Kerouac and Allen Ginsberg frequented coffeehouses like Café Wha? and The Gaslight Café, where some of the most profound artistic and literary works of the entire twentieth century were developed.

Greenwich Village's rich history extends far beyond its artistic legacy, of course. It was at the forefront of "scandalous" social movements such as women's suffrage and LGBTQ+ rights. In fact, it was in this neighborhood that the first gay rights organization in America, the Mattachine Society, was founded in 1950.

Today, Greenwich Village continues to be a vibrant hub for creativity and progressive thought. Its charming streets are lined with historic brownstones and iconic landmarks like Washington Square Park and Stonewall Inn. Despite undergoing gentrification in more recent years, Greenwich Village has managed to preserve its unique character while embracing modernity.

When Marty and Susan lived and worked in The Village, it was far removed from its farmland days. It remained an oasis for millions, however, who longed for the fertile soil of intellectual and artistic liberation. The subculture nurturance offered by The Village was a welcome wellspring for the Sackers.

Marty and Susan took out a modest New York City flat walking distance from The Village's Bleecker Street while Susan finished high school. She became involved in Northeastern regional theatre and toured as far as Maine with several little theatre productions. After she graduated in 1945, she mirrored Marty in taking on dual careers: artist by day, singer by night. With Susan's flourishing artistic talents, as an eighteen-year-old newlywed, she worked in an independent publishing house in Greenwich Village designing illustrations for children's books. She also snagged a nightly singing gig for The Village Barn's floorshow. Susan earned her spurs in drinking, smoking, and performing in one of the Northeast's most unique venues, described by *The Brooklyn Daily Eagle* as "New York's only *country* nightclub" (1939). The Village Barn was a renowned hotspot in which a number of well-knowns got their start, including Judy Canova, Don Cornell, and the Hartmans.

Susan was always of the short and slender persuasion, but in her youth, bony may have been a more accurate categorization, though "petite" was the more polite. Susan's black hair, brown eyes, and almost supernaturally perfect teeth had always been among her most arresting features. Her signature black hair had never known a pair of scissors until her mid-twenties. Hygienic luxuries such as haircuts hadn't been of priority in her transient childhood. As a teenager, when she first showed interest in cutting its thick length, one of the more conservative Catholic families she had been placed with vehemently opposed the "vain" inquiry. As a Greenwich Village hipster in the late 1940s, however, having jet black hair long enough to sit on was "cool" to the dive crowds of "alternative pop culture." The free-spirited artists of Greenwich Village often "scandalously" fostered many of America's counterculture movements. Artistically, socially, and politically, The Village was set apart with a guild vibe that became a haven for those, like Marty and Susan, who had something stuck in their blood they wanted to express and didn't have the sense of franchise within more traditional grids to do so.

Susan Cabot

The Village Barn was where "Susan Sacker" gave way to "Susan Cabot." Writer Trav S.D. theorized on her choice in stage names: "My guess is that her professional name is a kind of satirical eye-wink about her humble origins. The Cabots were one of the principal Boston Brahmin families, as distant from her own early circumstances as could be" (2022).

The Cabots were a prominent family in Boston during the eighteenth and nineteenth centuries, known for their involvement in various industries, including shipping, trade, and finance. The family played a significant role in the development of Boston's economy and helped establish the city as a major commercial center. Their wealth and influence allowed them to participate in philanthropic endeavors, vastly contributing to the growth and improvement of the city. Today, the Cabots are remembered as influential figures in Boston's history with a still-celebrated legacy. Susan chose a solid last name in reinventing herself, because who wouldn't want to be associated with a family like that?

Susan went on to attend college in New York, where she became even more captivated by the fine arts and humanities as she majored in music and art. In her music classes, she continued refining her voice and became proficient in the art of singing from a music theory perspective of performance. Music was a unifying entity for Susan, and something she remained passionate about throughout her life, often referring to it as "her first true love." "This thought has been expressed again and again, but it can never be said enough that music is a language common to all nations of the world," Susan said, "It transcends the barriers of politics and ideologies. The romance and the joy of life lie in being friends, and this is a sentiment best expressed in music."

In addition to her standing gig at The Village Barn, Susan sang in more traditional New York nightclubs—those without the wagon wheels and cowgirl routine. She embraced the sequined jazz scene of Greenwich in the late 1940s, giving her a well-rounded vocal seasoning. Whether they knew it or not, in "Susan Cabot," dive crowds were being entertained by an operatic hopeful, not just a cabaret pair of legs tied to a decent set of vocal cords. In her musical training, Susan's dream became to study opera in Italy, across the world from her childhood traumas and their forlorn residuals. She longed for so much more than her mother had in domestic survival. Susan was a creative spirit with infinite, operatic aspirations far beyond the impoverished silhouette of dishes and clotheslines she remembered consuming the households of all her foster placements.

The first few years of the Sackers' marriage were among the steadiest and most healing of Susan's whole life. The couple, like any, had their strained dynamics, but Susan had finally definitionally plateaued to "plenty." There were plenty of basic necessities, plenty of artistic opportunities, and plenty of "home" to push her beyond the mere survival of before. Marty wasn't perfect, but he sure beat the hell out of the gray slums of youth with their daily neglects and nightly abuses.

Chapter Two
California's No Italy, But It'll Do

"The first rule in opera is the first rule in life: see to everything yourself."
— Dame Nellie Melba

Through the Sackers' artistic connections, Susan was introduced to casting director Max Arnow who, throughout the Golden Era, became iconic in his work with A-listers like Ronald Reagan, Kim Novak, Shelley Winters, and Kay Francis. Arnow was also instrumental in casting for MGM's classic *Gone with the Wind.* It was nearly voltaic for Susan to be professionally pursued by him after he noticed her at The Village Barn. After all, he was the one who gave the world both Humphrey Bogart *and* Katherine Hepburn, so he knew talent and potential when he saw it.

In 1947, Arnow got Susan her first on-screen role. She played a "restaurant patron" at the Club 66 in Henry Hathaway's noir *Kiss of Death* for Twentieth Century Fox. Susan was technically an uncredited extra in the Oscar-nominated production, but shared the screen with Victor Mature and "newcomer" Richard Widmark. Several segments were filmed in New York, and Susan can be seen at a table next to the main characters while they use a Club 66 table in a tense exchange. Susan's profile and long, black hair are seen as she giggles over drinks with the men at her table. For a screen-green twenty-year-old, it was a start.

By 1950, Marty had transitioned from interior designer to full-time work with the Federal Security Agency while he continued freelancing as a painter. Susan continued in her illustrative work in the daytime and singing evenings at The Village Barn and other Greenwich Village nightspots. She also picked up another side gig as a jewelry designer for Gimbel's.

On May 24, 1948, The Village Barn made its television debut on NBC in a weekly variety show by the same name. The show was western-themed, like the venue and performances themselves, hosted by Zebe Carver, Dick Thomas, and Ray Forrest. The show featured special country-western guests along with house steadies, and Susan appeared in the ensemble. This fairly regular engagement with NBC landed her a few commercial roles in addition to the intermittent on-screen singing and dancing spots. She sang commercial drugstore themes for DuMont Television Network's jazzy and pseudo-vaudeville variety show *Cavalcade of Bands*.

Discovered Part II

After her film debut and string of television spots, by 1950, Susan had a more seasoned talent that stood out among The Village Barn performers. Hollywood producer Wallace MacDonald was patronizing the nightclub one evening when he, just as Max Arnow had, noticed Susan. MacDonald had a keen eye for what Hollywood and its audiences wanted, and with an upcoming film in the wings, he eyed Susan for a screen test.

It wasn't unusual for Hollywooders to frequent The Village Barn and to even make pitches and promises of grandeur to its performers occasionally, but Wallace MacDonald's pitch carried a greater density than some in 1950. He wasn't just a slick-talking talent scout with vague proposals, MacDonald approached Susan with a particular role. He wanted her for native girl "Moana" opposite Jon Hall in William Berke's *On the Isle of Samoa* for Columbia Pictures.

On the Isle of Samoa tells the story of former airman "Kenneth Crandall" (played by Jon Hall) who gets mixed up in a botched robbery at an Australian nightclub and barely escapes with the money. In his impromptu getaway, Crandall steals a plane, but soon crashes on an uncharted Samoan island called Tongaluha. He is befriended by the island's "Chief Tihoti" (played by Al Kikume), beautiful native girl, "Moana" (played by Susan Cabot), and the island's only other White man "Peter Appleton" (played by Raymond Greenleaf). While he falls in love with beautiful Moana, Crandall longs to return to civilization with his ill-gotten gain. Eventually, with the help of the islanders, he constructs an airstrip and repairs the damaged airplane and leaves lovestruck Moana behind.

It was a small role, but Susan knew film work, however scant in the beginning, could nudge her one step closer to becoming the world-renowned singer she longed to be. Marty was supportive despite his reservations about the flash of Hollywood, as M. Oakley Stafford with *The Hartford Courant* said, "[Marty] has confidence in [Susan], too, that's why the battle for her is half won. You win half of any battle at home."

Hollywood doesn't seem like an obvious next step for an aspiring opera singer, but some sources say just before Susan was discovered by MacDonald, she had been tentatively accepted into Milan's Teatro alla Scala (La Scala Theatre Ballet School) contingent upon a scholarship ironing out. She "settled" for Hollywood in the interim, but the scholarship to La Scala ultimately fell through. After accepting MacDonald's offer, Susan hoped to make enough money in film work to eventually reapply to La Scala when she could afford fare and tuition.

La Scala, also known as Teatro alla Scala, has for centuries been considered one of the most prestigious opera houses in the world. Located in Milan, Italy, it has a gilded history that dates back to 1778, when it was officially inaugurated. Designed by neoclassical architect Giuseppe Piermarini, La Scala's pilastered building has become synonymous with traditional magnificence in opera and ballet. Susan longed to bask in the theater's opulence as an operatic principal, having her voice ricochet through the golden and red velveted halls. Susan's dreams of La Scala's stage were never realized, but even today the theatre continues to be a symbol of artistic brilliance and continues to attract audiences from around the globe with its live, classical programming.

MacDonald gave Susan a mouth-watering "perhaps" that cinched the deal. Having been captivated not only by her beauty, but also her accomplished vocal talent, MacDonald suggested that even though *On the Isle of Samoa* didn't offer a true singing role, "perhaps" other screen roles in the future would. That "perhaps" helped her convince Marty and pack their bags. Susan was used to packing up and changing directions, so she and Marty temporarily left their New York City settlement for her first real introduction to Hollywood lights.

Splintering on the West Coast

Marty and Susan relocated to Los Angeles for several months during the filming of *On the Isle of Samoa* after the old screen test routine. The Sackers were given fare to get to the West Coast, but they were initially on their own for accommodations. They took out a little studio apartment on the fringe of Los Angeles and scrimped on meals in "playing Hollywood" during the production. It was uncomfortable for them both, but terribly exciting for Susan. Unfortunately, for Marty, it was all too phony.

Though supportive of Susan's aspirations, he preferred the stability of what they had together in New York without the gamble of "machined-Hollywood" and risk of cheapening their beloved artistic interests.

In 1950, Marty, twenty-eight, and Susan, twenty-four, were young but had been seasoned by the artistic training and guild climate of Manhattan. Hollywood was a gaudy world of novelty compared to their raw, urban craftsmanship. Marty could be sulky and terse with Susan's artistic "compromise" in playing the lovestruck, few-lined role of exotic "Moana" — something he crassly equated to a burlesque mimic.

Susan, on the other hand, though she was new to the specific rules, knew Hollywood's game had to be played in order to see eventual results. More skeptical and with less patience than Susan, Marty didn't want to even try learning the rules. Milan would have offered both Sackers legions of opportunities if Susan had been able to attend La Scala, but Hollywood? That was an altogether different sociocultural climate that didn't offer the same traditional artistic nurturing they were each really looking for. This caused their marriage to fray under the façade Los Angeles expected. They used nearly every cent they had to invest in their stay with the slim hope of Susan snagging a contract beyond the role of "dusky, sarong-wrapped Moana." With the help of MacDonald's motivational campaigns, Susan believed their initial investment would eventually be worth it ten times over, but Marty wasn't so easily convinced. Marty (and on some level Susan too) found Hollywood's razzled strategy for young, attractive newcomers like Susan a bit insulting to both their training and aspirations as serious artists.

Marty and Susan's relationship became increasingly strained during their initial West Coast relocation. Friends watched over their home in New York while they were away, but much to his frustration, Marty's work there had been put on hold in this Hollywood "investment venture." Marty's skepticism wasn't altogether unfounded because *On the Isle of Samoa* turned out to be the beginning of a tumble of similar, linear B-movie roles for Susan. In his increasingly detached support of her during filming, Susan accused Marty of sheer snobbery while he accused her of cheapening their dreams, in a sarong of all things.

Despite her own doubts in MacDonald's pitches and promises after seeing Hollywood's price tag (both literally and figuratively) Susan got caught up in the fanfare of it all. She became captivated by the siren song of what she could be within Hollywood's gloried context of potential. Filming for Twentieth Century Fox had been thrilling despite the considered shallowness of "Moana's" role, though years later Susan said of her performance in *On the Isle of Samoa*: "It was terrible, and I was terrible. I played a sarong girl. I was so cute you could have killed me. You know, one of those cute little monsters just bubbling over all over the place."

The publicity tour MacDonald secured around her was also enthralling with appearances, photo shoots, and newspaper mentions helping to establish her brand as "Susan Cabot, rising Hollywood starlet."

Marty was a bit lost in the flashbulbs of it all, and as the two drifted further apart in the sea of studio promises that seemed to fall through on technicalities, he brooded over the secretly held fear that Susan had merely used him as a convenient vehicle to escape the cycle of trauma and poverty in The Bronx foster care. And maybe unconsciously she did, in so much as all of us "use" love to become more of who we are supposed to be, but

Susan idolized Marty in a sense. Whether either one had intentionally viewed their marriage as a rescue operation initially, Marty had, in fact, been her savior. Her early days developed in her a great sense of loyalty to Marty that was difficult to shake despite their differences. He had, in a way, "raised her" from a survivalistic seventeen-year-old orphan to an aspiring operatic that just happened to detour through Hollywood on the way to Milan.

Taking on Hollywood Alone

The 1950s in America was a period of significant sociopolitical, economic, and cultural transformation. It was a time of post-war prosperity and optimism, with the country experiencing a booming economy and a growing middle class. The decade saw the rise of consumer culture, with Americans embracing new technologies and products in the "space age." Suburbs flourished as families moved out of cities and into newly built "ranch-style" (some of which were prefabricated) homes. The 1950s were also marked by "The Baby Boom" that led to a population explosion in the aftermath of World War II. More than four million babies were born annually from 1954 to 1964, creating the generation known as "The Baby Boomers." The Beat Generation also emerged from the cultural landscape of the 1950s, of which Susan's beloved Greenwich Village became the nucleus.

The 1950s also birthed the beginnings of sociopolitical movements such as the civil rights movement, as African Americans and other marginalized groups fought for equality and an end to segregation. The second wave of feminism began to stir on issues of reproductive rights, workplace discrimination, and domestic violence, priming American culture for the coming shifts in traditional gender roles.

Popular culture was dominated by the emergence of rock and roll music, the rise of television, and the influence of Hollywood. Overall, the 1950s in America was a time of progress and prosperity, and the cultural landscape of the country and the world was reflected on the silver screen.

The second wave of the Red Scare of the 1940s and 1950s was a period of intense paranoia about communism's spread in the United States. This rampant paranoia that often gave way to hysterics was fueled by the belief that communist spies and sympathizers had infiltrated American society, particularly within the government and entertainment industry. The United States government launched investigations and hearings to detect suspected communists through Senator Joseph McCarthy's infamous interrogation initiatives. This resulted in the blacklisting of hundreds of people who had their careers and sometimes entire lives destroyed. Hollywood was a choice target for McCarthyism hysterics that led to the blacklisting of actors and actresses of all varieties. As a B-list starlet, the Red Scare seemed to pass over Susan without attempts to tie her personal and professional activities to communism, but dozens of her colleagues weren't so lucky.

The significant cultural changes of the 1950s impacted Hollywood's industry and deliverables. The rise of television posed a major threat to the dominance of cinema as audiences began to stay at home to watch their favorite shows. In response, Hollywood sought to lure viewers back into theaters by experimenting with innovative technologies, such as 3D and widescreen formats (including CinemaScope). These technologies helped to transform both production and exhibition practices that gave audiences larger-than-life immersive experiences in theatres. Additionally, color film became more widely available, leading to a shift away from traditional black-and-white cinematography.

Another important development during this period was the rise of independent filmmaking (Roger Corman, anyone?). In response to increased studio control over content and production, many filmmakers began to work outside the old Hollywood studio system, creating their own production companies or forming alliances with other like-minded artists. This led to an increase in artistic freedom and experimentation, as filmmakers were no longer bound by commercial considerations. This also led to the eventual breakdown of the exploitative old Hollywood studio system and its corporate ownership of stars.

In terms of genres, Hollywood in the 1950s witnessed a resurgence in on-screen musicals. Films such as Stanley Donen's *Singin' in the Rain* (1952) and Vincente Minnelli's *An American in Paris* (1951) (both of which starred Gene Kelly) showcased elaborate song-and-dance numbers that captivated audiences through the high-quality entertainment and escapism they offered. The 1950s was a decade marked by social change, industrial expansion, and the emergence of the "space-age."

However, not all films produced during this era were light-hearted musicals. The 1950s also saw the emergence of film noir, a genre characterized by its dark and cynical portrayal of post-war America. Films like William Dieterle's *The Turning Point* (1952) and Fritz Lang's *The Big Heat* (1953) explored themes of corruption, betrayal, and moral ambiguity, reflecting the uncertainties of the time.

Further, Hollywood faced mounting pressure from governmental entities that were concerned about the influence films had on society. This led to stricter enforcement of the Production Code, a set of guidelines that regulated content in films. While these restrictions limited artistic freedom in some ways, they also forced filmmakers to find creative ways to address controversial topics within the confines of censorship. Despite challenges posed by television competition and censorship regulations, Hollywood continued to captivate audiences with its ability to both entertain and address societal concerns through its grand productions.

Another defining feature of Hollywood in the 1950s was the emergence of Lee Strasberg's method acting. Actors such as Marlon Brando and James Dean brought a new dimension of realism to their performances in abandoning more traditional theatrical techniques in favor of Strasberg's naturalistic approach. This style of acting, which emphasized emotional authenticity and psychological depth, had a profound influence on subsequent generations of actors—but the method was admittedly not Susan Cabot's cup of tea. Marlon Brando himself, for a time, *was* Susan's cup of tea, but after he suggested she come to his side of the fence with regard to the reformist approach, she found Meisner's traditional means of performing to be much more appealing.

***

After seven years of marriage, Marty and Susan separated at the end of 1950. The two stayed in touch despite his move back to New York, unable to reach an agreement on future plans fair to them both. The perpetual cold stalemate led to emotional fallouts that became unbearable, and Susan filed for divorce in March of 1952. With her dark features and perfect figure, Susan didn't stay single long. While she was seen with many dashing escorts, many of whom were Hollywood A-listers, most of the reported rendezvous were just for publicity and casual nightlife amusement. She was very selective in her serious romantic pursuits and kept most of her dates at a satin-gloved arm's length, contrary to what Hollywood columnists led readers to believe.

It was much easier for Susan to navigate the Hollywood social scene as a single gal than it was being married to an uninvolved anti-Hollywooder. Susan's budding visibility, thanks to Twentieth Century Fox, began bringing in more invitations than money at first. Susan was seen at nearly every major Hollywood party of the early 1950s, often on the arms of Hollywood's most sought-after Casanovas. *The Los Angeles Mirror* reported that Susan was dating Rock Hudson in January 1951 in a publicity push for their film *Tomahawk*. Hollywood columnists often reported spotting her at a variety of posh Beverly Hills parties and Sunset Blvd. nightclubs with the likes of Scott Brady, Tom Drake, Jackie Barnett, Arthur Loew Jr., Hugh O'Brian, and Marlon Brando.

Tumble of the 1950s

In December of 1950, just as Marty and Susan were separating, Bill Goetz signed Susan under a seven-year contract with Universal-International Pictures. Universal-International was where Susan really earned her sea legs in acting, even though the roles given to her weren't exactly top-of-the-line leads. She told *The Montreal Star* about her career before being a contract player: "I hadn't any idea how to act, but all I did anyway was run around the beach in a sarong."

Under contract, she first appeared in George Sherman's Western drama *Tomahawk* with Van Heflin, Yvonne De Carlo, and Rock Hudson. Susan's character, "Monahseetah," is a Sioux Indian girl who holds a pivotal plot twist in relations between the Sioux and the United States Cavalry. As usual, Susan took her supporting role very seriously. With coaching from John War Eagle, who plays "Red Cloud" in the film, Susan learned the Sioux language. She told journalist Lucille Mabbott, "Learning to speak lines in Sioux was not difficult for I have had to have a nodding acquaintance with several languages while studying opera." Because of her portrayal as "Monahseetah," she was adopted as an honorary Sioux and given the name "Ishta Washteh Winyan," which means "pretty eyes woman."

Much of *Tomahawk* was filmed in Black Hills, South Dakota, and in promotion of the production, the cast appeared at the Alex Johnson Hotel in Rapid City in a farewell variety show performance. Susan had a few soprano solos at the publicity event, including "Who Cares?" from *Of Thee I Sing*, and "Bali Hai" from *South Pacific*. She was given superb reviews in the papers by both the audience and her fellow cast members.

Famed columnist Hedda Hopper said, "Bill Goetz signed Susan Cabot for an acting part in *Tomahawk, then* discovered that she sings—but beautifully. He may dust off one of Deanna Durbin's old pictures and remake it with her." Things were looking propitious for Susan with looming prophesies of big-scale success, perhaps even in both acting *and* singing.

Shortly after *Tomahawk*, Susan was cast in Warner Brothers' 1951 film *The Enforcer* starring Humphrey Bogart, Zero Mostel, and Ted de Corsia. In this film noir, Susan plays the uncredited role of crime victim "Nina Lombardo." Bretaigne Windust and Raoul Walsh directed the production that featured Susan more in reference than actual screen time. Still, having shared the screen with demigod Humphrey Bogart wasn't a bad gig for a starlet rising from the wings of supporting roles.

Susan's next film was Arabian adventure *The Prince Who Was a Thief*, starring Tony Curtis and Piper Laurie. Rudolph Maté's *The Prince Who Was a Thief* is based on writer Theodore Dreiser's short story of thirteenth-century Tangiers, in which assassin "Yussef" (played by Everett Sloane) is sent to kill the next in line for the throne: baby Prince Hussein. Yussef second-guesses his mission and keeps the royal child "Julna" (played by Tony Curtis) to raise. Unaware of his imperial blood, Julna grows up to become a thief like the man he believes to be his father. Susan had a small, uncredited role in the Rudolph Maté film, but it was the first of two starring the Curtis and Laurie duo that would later influence public opinion on Susan's personal involvement with real-life foreign dignitary King Hussein of Jordan.

In Kurt Neumann's romantic-adventure film *Son of Ali Baba* (1952), Tony Curtis portrays "Kashma Baba," the son of infamous Arabian hero "Ali Baba," with Piper Laurie as "Princess Azura of Fez, Kiki," his central love interest. "Kashma" is a dedicated Persian military cadet, but a perennial playboy in his personal life. The film tells the story of "Kashma's" brushes with love and rivalry within the shadow cast by his father's legacy. Susan plays the supporting character "Tala," one of the many Arabian beauties enamored with "Kashma." The film was produced by Leonard Goldstein in tandem with Universal Pictures, but it wasn't necessarily a blockbuster. Curtis and Laurie had starred together in a similar production (also featuring Susan Cabot), *The Prince Who Was a Thief* (1951), and after their electric on-screen match, fans wanted to see the couple take on more Arabian adventures together, and Kurt Neumann delivered. Both films were fairly forgettable, except for Tony Curtis' famously misquoted line in *Son of Ali Baba*: "In yonder valley lies the castle of my father," when the line in actuality is, "This is my father's palace, and yonder lies the Valley of the Sun." Neither Arabian adventure film was a masterstroke production, but in light of how Susan's off-screen romantic intrigues played out just a few years after, *The Prince Who Was a Thief* and *Son of Ali Baba* became compelling on a different octave.

Despite the tumble of Universal-International film roles in the early 1950s, Susan didn't forget her theatrical roots. In August 1952, she starred in Phillip Barry's hit *Second Threshold* in a six-night run at the Laguna Summer Theatre. This hiatus into little theatre helped nurture Susan's traditional artistic needs outside of the somewhat shallow roles her studio contract had granted her. Studio pay wasn't bad, though, at $175 a week, which today would be nearly $6,000 a month.

Whether on stage or screen, Susan took her roles seriously, even when they weren't exactly Shakespeare. In 1952, George Sherman requested Susan for *The Battle at Apache Pass*. Sherman's classic Western, starring John Lund, follows the tribes of Chief Cochise (played by Jeff Chandler) and Geronimo (played by Jay Silverheels) in their complex frontier relations with the United States Army. The film is largely based on the accounts of both "The Bascom Affair of 1861" and the real "Battle of Apache Pass of 1862."

In preparing for the role of Chief Cochise's wife, "Nona," Susan learned how to shoot a bow and arrow. National champion female archer Babe Bitzenberger, who was considered the "Annie Oakley of archery" in the 1940s, coached Susan. She used her training in two 1952 films of very different genres: *The Battle at Apache Pass* and *Son of Ali Baba*.

With several films under her belt, Susan became a favorite topic of newspapers on both the East and West Coast, though most were fluffy fanfare features about how she kept her skin so flawless or how she managed to stay in shape. For all the dripping glamor of her LA life, Susan appreciated a minimalist, organic approach to self-care. Papers loved to share her "secrets" with fans, including her egg yolk facials, lemon juice foot baths, and oil of almond body lotion.

Susan's greatest suggestion to maintain one's beauty was found in the healing properties of rest. "I've watched people who are tired, and it doesn't matter how carefully their hair is dressed or how much make-up they have on—the first thing you see in their face is fatigue," she told columnist Lydia Lane.

> *It's not always easy to get rest, but I'm trying to learn to go through the day accomplishing just as much with less energy. This means I must never rush, because the moment I do, my muscles tense and energy is thrown away… The important thing is to be alerted to fatigue signals.*

It means learning to take a break when it can do the most good. Efficiency experts have proved that only a few moments of rest at the right time renews your energy, your enthusiasm, and makes it possible for you to think or work more effectively. People who drive themselves, who won't stop a minute, are actually defeating their own purpose. They would reach their goal faster and more efficiently if they would learn how to conserve energy.

One series of self-care tips Susan gave to the masses through *The Los Angeles Times* in 1958 eventually became one of the most haunting in light of her murder twenty-eight years later. There was a half-page spread on "How to Look Your Best," according to pretty, fit actress Susan Cabot. Each photo shows Susan holding barbells in various positions to "sit and stretch for figure flattery." In one photo, Susan is seen holding the barbell against the back of her neck for exercises targeting the chest and waist. "Begin with knees bent near chest, then slowly straighten legs. Return to bent position. Do only five times to start. You'll find weight at neck prevents shoulders and arms from helping with the pulling and stretching," the article suggests.

***

When she traveled on publicity tours for many of her films, she enjoyed personally connecting with fans and donating her appearances and her own studio salary to causes across the nation and the world.

Susan held such staunch appreciation for all worldviews and ways of life, but was especially proud of her own American heritage. "The sentiment is common among the artists that we are citizens first, and as such we should do everything to preserve the American way of life," she said. In 1953, Susan made a short film for the United States Department of the Treasury called *The Bond Between Us* in support of war bonds.

Susan was also tremendously passionate about children's charities long before she became a mother herself, and enjoyed visiting with children within the organizations she supported while touring. She was involved with the March of Dimes, which was still a fairly new organization in the 1950s, the Maryland Society for Crippled Children, children's hospitals in nearly every state, and the establishments closest to her own impoverished childhood: orphanages.

The La Crosse Sunday Tribune did a full feature on Susan's visit to Wisconsin's La Crosse Home for Children in March of 1953. Susan leisurely spent an entire day at the orphanage reading books to the children, singing with them, and teaching a few to play the piano. She had a rolling pile of babies and toddlers in her lap throughout the day. One little boy named Johnny Day especially impressed her with his piano skills when he played Chopin's "Love in My Heart," to which she sang along. When the fun day with the pretty movie star came to an end, Susan gave Johnny a special treat: a red lipstick print that nearly covered his entire cheek. He swore he would never wash his cheek again until the house mother, Miss Josephine Fletcher, changed his mind. She had him wash it off before bed that night because it wouldn't do to have a movie star's lip print on his cheek for Sunday school the next morning.

Under Contract

From 1950 to 1954, Susan was cast in seven films under Universal-International contract. The films all seemed to blur together in their similarities and generally lesser-known status despite some A-lister leads. Susan was "type-cast" as "dark, exotic little things" in Westerns, noirs, or exotic adventure films, with generally few lines and incidental screen time. Some of those seven film roles she even had to lobby for:

> *I had five ulcers before they let me play Jeff Chandler's Indian wife in The Battle of Apache Pass. They said that Jeff was too tall for me. I went running around from office to office politicking for the part. I reminded them that Helen Hayes had played with Gary Cooper in Farewell to Arms and that the picture was one of Hollywood's greatest love stories.*

Susan's persistence only afforded her contractual appearances in one-dimensional roles that she was often embarrassed by, like the role of "Clio," the Corsican spitfire in *Flame of Araby* whose central purpose was to provide dignitaries with a "cooch dance" that she described as something "censors [would] probably cut [it]. I was told to go from side to side only, but I forgot. You can't describe circles on the screen with your hips."

Charles Lamont's *Flame of Araby* tells the story of lovely Arabian Princess Tanya (played by Maureen O'Hara) who feuds with Bedouin chief "Tamerlane" (played by Jeff Chandler) over ownership of a prized stallion. They quickly put their differences aside, however, to unite in opposition of their mutual enemies: the Corsair Lords. Susan portrays the role of palace dancer "Clio." *Flame of Araby* was the first of two films Susan performed in with heartthrob Jeff Chandler.

Part of Susan's typecast stagnation (in a whitewashing sense) was also because she refused casting couch offers that came her way. Author Laura Wagner said, "Universal basically saw Cabot as either an exotic or a tomboy," which did little to cultivate her voice or her self-confidence in being taken seriously by the industry. Susan became frustrated after the many back-to-back roles that not only failed to showcase her voice but also her artistic potential as a serious actress. At 5'2 and 95lbs, Susan said, "I'm either in jungles or gypsy wagons. I don't know why. My coloring is exactly like Elizabeth Taylor's. Do they put her in a sarong? No!"

One of the casting difficulties Susan perpetually came up against was her "pint-sized" stature. *The News and Observer* referred to her as "short but determined." She said in the *Long Beach Press-Telegram* that it is only fun to be tiny when you've reached the top… "Until then, it's a real pain in the neck." Her height blurred producers' view of her ability:

> *I felt like kicking or screaming every time a producer told me I'd be great in a part except that I was too little. I began getting a midget complex the second month I was in Hollywood. I had a stock spiel for producers. I reminded them that nobody speaks of Helen Hayes anymore as 'that short actress.' They only consider her stature as an artist. After all, some small people have done some mighty big things, men and women alike. The history of show business is full of instances of personalities of whom*

the critics thought no less because they were half-pints. Take the late Maude Adams, as an example, among yesterday's stars, and Bette Davis as one among today's.

Susan became increasingly impatient with Universal-International, partially on grounds of inequity, as *The Valley Times* surmised: Susan's "formula for her tough climb to stardom, she said, was to wage a continuous battle against discrimination." For months, she showed up every day at noon in Universal's commissary as a living, breathing commercial for directors and producers who might happen to see her physical credentials and availability. Columnist Jack Gaver said in his famed critic column "Up and Down Broadway" in 1952:

The studio has brought her along gradually, but now the pressure is on to make her a big name in short order. Her chief desire is to get into a picture in which she won't have to play an Indian or Western girl.

Finally, Universal-International gave her semi-leads in three Westerns opposite Audie Murphy: *The Duel at Silver Creek* (1952), *Gunsmoke* (1953), and *Ride Clear of Diablo* (1954). She and Murphy enjoyed working together, as evidenced by their charming on-screen chemistry. Susan joked that the only reason Universal-International kept her on its payroll was to be Murphy's leading lady because who else could they find shorter than he was? "Being short on height, [at 5'5] Audie requires the romantic services of an actress [Susan] who won't dwarf him by comparison," *The Valley Times* printed of the duo. "I keep right on plugging for Audie to make more pictures because that means I hang onto my job here just that much longer," Susan said.

Often playing the valiant but edgy hero on-screen, Audie Murphy became a highly decorated American soldier before entering the film industry. Born on June 20, 1925, in Kingston, Texas, Audie enlisted in the United States Army at the age of seventeen. During World War II, he served in the European theater and earned numerous medals for his bravery and valor, including the Medal of Honor. After the war, Audie transitioned into a successful acting career, starring in over forty films. He was well-known for his rugged good looks and intense performances, primarily in

Westerns and war dramas. Audie Murphy's contributions to both the military and film industry have made him an American icon. He is remembered as the most decorated American soldier of WWII.

Like Susan, Audie also met with a tragic and untimely death. On May 28, 1971, Audie and five others boarded a private plane in Atlanta, Georgia, headed for Martinsville, Virginia. The two-engine Aero Commander 680 Super was a small, private plane owned and operated by Colorado Aviation. The pilot reportedly took a chance on dubious weather conditions before takeoff. During the flight, the pilot lost their sense of spatial orientation due to the dense rain and fog. Only an hour away from their destination, the plane crashed into the side of Brush Mountain. Despite the valiant efforts of the pilot and crew, there were no survivors. Audie was forty-six years old. In 1974, the Veterans of Foreign Wars erected a monument in commemoration of Audie and his fellow air travelers who lost their lives in the plane crash.

Despite his eventual movie star status, Audie remained an unwavering advocate for military men and women who, like himself, bore the scars of wartime and were suddenly sent back home with few resources. He was one of the first to publicly acknowledge the difficulties soldiers had in re-acclimating to civilian life: "After the war, they took army dogs and rehabilitated them for civilian life," Audie said, "but they turned soldiers into civilians immediately and let 'em sink or swim." Audie's personal and professional legacies are unmatched, as he not only served his country with distinction but also made significant contributions to the entertainment industry. When news of his death flew through the papers, Susan was teary-eyed for days, just like millions of other Audie Murphy admirers around the globe. Though the papers loved to hint at off-screen romantic interludes between Susan and Audie, the two were more like good pals than anything else.

Don Siegel's 1952 Western drama *The Duel at Silver Creek* was Susan's most expansive on-screen role to that point in her career. While personally she wasn't an avid Western fan, her familiarity with the novelty of Westerns in pop culture began in Greenwich Village, of all places. She learned the ropes of portraying the stereotypical "cowgirl" when she sang at The Village Barn in her late teens and early twenties. The on-screen chemistry between Susan and Audie led to the three other films they did together, plus the idea of another that got canned before production.

Siegel's *The Duel at Silver Creek* stars Audie Murphy as "Silver Kid," a young gunslinger seeking revenge for his father's murder. Tomboy "Jane 'Dusty' Fargo" (played by Susan Cabot) joins the Silver Kid in his pursuit of the murderous claim jumpers and ends up falling for the brave avenger. This film was the first of Don Siegel's Western films, and the first of three Susan and Audie performed in together.

In the second of their Western films together, Nathan Juran's 1953 *Gunsmoke,* Susan and Audie again face the lawless frontier. Audie stars as "Reb Kittridge," a hired gun sent to obtain deeds from ranchers who have refused to sell out to the land-hungry "Matt Telford" (played by Donald Randolph). When Reb approaches the ranch of "Dan Saxon," he discovers that the rancher's lovely daughter, "Rita" (played by Susan Cabot), is perhaps more important than his original charge as a hired killer.

Despite its name, there was no connection between the film and the long-running television and radio shows that were also named *Gunsmoke*. Fans often confused the film with the long-running television series starring James Arness, and would tell Susan how much they enjoyed her in "that Matt Dillon show."

The third and final Western Susan did with Audie was Jesse Hibbs' *Ride Clear of Diablo.* Audie portrays yet another frontier avenger in the film with Susan as his love interest. Railroad man "Clay O'Mara" seeks revenge on the corrupt political figures who murdered his father. Susan's character, "Laurie Kenyon," aids O'Mara on his journey toward vindication.

The Face of Minorities

Even though Susan's contract work wasn't terribly fulfilling for her, nor did it plunge her to the heights of the A-list, her portrayals of female minorities in "exotic roles" of island girls, Native Americans, and women of

Eastern ethnicity were actually quite progressive for the 1940s and 1950s—certainly not progressive by postmodern standards today, but during an era in which there was virtually no diversity represented on-screen at all, Susan became one of the first stand-ins for women of minority.

The first Native American woman to appear in a film was Lilian St. Cyr, known professionally as "Princess Red Wing" in 1914. Though her first several performances were in silent films, Lilian went on to perform in major talkies and directed and produced several films with her husband, James Young Deer. Lilian and James embraced some of their ethnic stereotype roles not because they agreed with them, but because they felt it was a first step toward eventually broadening them to accuracy.

For most of the twentieth century, the sociopolitical climate of America would not allow female minorities to tell their own stories through their own ethnically corresponding characters, a practice that still occurs today and is often referred to as "whitewashing." Susan's supporting roles under contract may not have won her Oscars, but her portrayals of women of minorities were, in retrospect, far more significant than perhaps she realized for that era.

Susan became the visual representation of female Japanese, Native American, and Samoan characters who were often acknowledged only by general description rather than by name in 1940s and 1950s entertainment. Susan was one of the few supporting actresses who (slowly) helped inch open Hollywood's door of acceptance for women in underrepresented people groups.

George Sherman's 1951 film *Tomahawk*, in which Susan portrayed Monahseetah, was lauded as a progressive feat for the industry at the time. In the United Kingdom, *Tomahawk* was released under the title *Battle of Powder River* despite the real Battle of Powder River occurring in a completely different location and time period than the events dramatized in *Tomahawk*. "The Red Indian has been badly mauled both in fact and fiction. Here is a film that seeks to repair the injustice with an attempt to stick to the truth," *Picturegoer*'s Alan R. Warwick reported of the film's February

1951 release, along with a full page shot of Susan as the beautiful "Monahseetah."

Warwick also acknowledged the film industry's history of whitewashing, and further reported:

With that nation's growing awareness of their earlier treatment of the Indians as a soiled page in that history, it is to their credit that they have made this new film without a garnishing of the earlier popular habit of whitewashing the white men and daubing to crimson the red men. In fact, this film sincerely attempts to portray the men of the period as they were, not sparing the white men in revealing their broken promises, their ruthless greed, and their blood lust. It is a film made with a conscience.

In the *Schirmer Encyclopedia of Film*, Professor of Anthropology at the University of New Mexico, Beverly R. Singer, argues that:

Despite the fact that a diversity of indigenous peoples had a legal and historical significance in the formation of every new country founded in the Western Hemisphere, in the United States and Canada, the term 'Indians' became a hegemonic designation implying that they were all the same in regards to culture, behavior, language, and social organization.

It wasn't until 1990, when Kevin Costner's *Dances with Wolves* was released, fifty years after Susan's contract work, that audiences were given more positive and comprehensive representations of Native American people.

Singer says:

Representations of Native Americans in popular film are as interesting as they are problematic: the subject remains somewhat static as the other, while the position of the producer of such texts—mainly the Euro-American majority—has undergone a drastic shift in the last five decades, according to 'Native American Identity in Popular Film, 1950-Present.'

There are countless points of view with regard to this discussion, and some film historians disagree with Singer's interpretation in their reference to early films that show a wide range of depictions of Native Americans in their nobility, integrity, and grit. Though film has been fraught with narrow stereotyping of nearly every people group in the world, both majority and minority alike, the examination of Susan's contribution to the overall interpretation of diversity is interesting, no matter where one falls on the spectrum of perspectives.

Today, many on-screen depictions of the underrepresented are considered archaic and insulting, but considering the context of early film, the inclusion of minorities sometimes offered a different worldview to a sea dominated by the White perspective. Susan was one of the first faces White majority audiences associated with other ethnicities and other ways of life. She was a visual liaison between women of various people groups and an American culture that historically had not been comfortable with *different*.

Even in 1973, nearly twenty years after Susan's portrayals of women minorities, the film industry still exhibited a staunch bias toward actors, actresses, and themes that were not representative of the White majority. Everyone remembers the infamous Oscar night when Marlon Brando (one of Susan Cabot's on-and-off suitors) snubbed the Academy and his peers over the industry's discriminatory treatment of Native Americans. Through his friend, actress and activist, Maria Louise Cruz, known by her stage name "Sacheen Littlefeather," Brando refused to accept the Oscar he won for his performance in *The Godfather*. Littlefeather made a brief statement on his behalf when his win was announced, but crowds were less than sympathetic toward her sociopolitical platform. Many booed and hissed at her, and many top celebrities reportedly charged the stage and even confronted her after the ceremony with disparaging remarks. Littlefeather was blacklisted after that night at the Oscars, but continued her activism as a "Native icon."

Almost fifty years after the harassment Littlefeather endured that night, the Academy issued a public apology to her and to all Native Americans who had been ostracized by mainstream industry positions and productions. Unfortunately, Littlefeather died just weeks after the apology came at age seventy-six. Since her death, her family has accused her of being an "ethnic fraud" in her longtime claim of being Apache. Littlefeather's sisters came forward with new information about their family heritage. Rosalind Cruz and Trudy Orlandi say that their family originated from Mexico, and "Littlefeather" was simply a nickname for their sister. "It's a fraud," Cruz said to *The San Francisco Chronicle* in 2022: "It's disgusting to the heritage of the tribal people. And it's just insulting to my parents." Nobody likes to be tricked, of course, but regardless of Littlefeather's true ethnicity, her activism was significant for Native Americans, namely women, in film and perhaps in the world. Though Susan Cabot may not have considered herself an intentional activist, her work to reflect women of many different ethnic groups during a narrow era is certainly noteworthy.

Before American audiences of the 1940s and 1950s were introduced to film and television depictions of minorities, directors used casting mnemonics to "prime" majority audiences to the "scandalous" idea of seeing different types of people groups being represented within their *own* stories. In other words, it was somehow more palatable for the White majority to see a White woman tell the story of a Native American. Before more realistic casting practices became the norm, Native American characters were often played by Caucasian actors or actresses (or in Susan's case, a Russian-Jewish woman) who could either be easily made to appear Native American or happened to already possess associated physical characteristics. Susan's Russian-Jewish heritage, dark hair, dark eyes, and slender frame made her a frequent choice for supporting roles under contract with Universal-International.

Ride Clear of Diablo would be her last film with Universal-International. Even before signing on for her third film with Murphy, there were press rumblings of a career divorce between Susan and Universal-International. The studio was content repeating the same formulaic films for her, but she was restless and longed for more artistic challenge.

New York Again

For four years Susan believed if she just held out long enough, her offers would improve. The cyclical nature of that belief has snagged many a fine people—that siren's song gamble that *surely* the next one will be different. But of course, it wasn't. "I have so many other things I like to do besides making pictures," Susan said in an interview with *The Boston Globe*. "I want to paint. I would like a concert career, and I would even like grand opera. But that last one, I realize, is silly since it would mean three years of doing nothing but train. And then I want to write too," she said.

Susan officially broke away from Universal-International in 1954. There wasn't a dramatic reason with a corresponding dramatic exit as many theorized, though the papers certainly hinted at such. Susan's salary, like many starlets in her "newcomer" studio class, earned a hard $175 a week with little room for raise negotiation. Susan's friend and *Creature from the Black Lagoon* star Lori Nelson parted ways with Universal- International around the same time Susan did because she refused to continue under contract without the pay raise executives gave "men and A-list dolls." Though the non-existent raises were reason enough for some to mutiny, the larger issue for Susan was the types of roles she had been pigeon-holed into—roles that did not showcase her singing voice.

When Susan and several other Hollywood starlets got out from under studio reign in the 1950s, it wasn't within the context of accepted female empowerment. Nearly all industries, including Hollywood, have been guilty of the misogynistic practices of unequal pay and unequal treatment of their contract players contingent upon gender. White men have always been of greater preference in terms of opportunity and compensation, but women (especially B-listers) have long since been hirable by their appearance, measurements (that were often printed in the newspapers in the Golden Era), availability, and how willing they were to submit to the studio system's dominion.

Under the rule of studio kingpins, working conditions, especially for women, were often at best uncomfortable and at worst completely exploitative and unsafe. We've all heard the horror stories of what the studio system did to its stars like Judy Garland, Joan Crawford, Lana Turner, and Ava Gardner, with forced abortions and coverups of all varieties. Studios carefully worded their contracts to use as licenses to a star's mind, body, and soul. Female stars were given weight mandates, steady streams of "pep pills" to stay amped for hours and hours of filming with few breaks, and a general dictator-like micromanagement of their private and professional lives. Though B actresses didn't typically experience the same overt micromanaging that A actresses did, they certainly all had their share of humiliations and dehumanization.

From roughly 1927 to 1950, the studio system gave the world some of the most prolific films in history, but at a wretched cost for many of Hollywood's female creatives, from the uncredited stunt double to the A-lister starlet, with Susan somewhere in the middle.

Perhaps due in part to her fragmented childhood fraught with transition, Susan was a flight risk when things got uncomfortable. If something wasn't working either in a relationship or in her career, she just *left* and channeled that severing into betterment for the next thing. That type of self-preservation strategy was completely foreign to Hollywood. Most starlets instinctually bowed to the patriarchy of directors and producers and compromised until they bled, but not Susan.

Susan hopped the next plane to New York as soon as she got out from under Universal-International's fist and committed herself to rigorous training she hoped would eventually translate to an "improvement" that either Broadway or Hollywood would surely notice, or perhaps even La Scala's admissions board.

In 1954, a twenty-seven-year-old Susan flew "home" to New York City and reconnected with what the urban arts had to offer after four years of Hollywood's technicolor hues and flashbulb headaches. Her first stop was the Actors' Studio and its innovative "method" acting. She supposedly "took three looks at it" and jumped ship for the traditional likes of Sanford Meisner, "who [had] more sensible ideas about acting."

She studied under Meisner for a year at the Neighborhood Playhouse and resumed her operatic voice lessons. She landed several stage roles during her rebound trip and somewhat angry determination to "be better." In September of 1954, Susan appeared with Philip Pine in the off-Broadway *A Stone for Danny Fisher* at the Downtown National Theatre on lower Second Ave. In July of 1955, she played "Hero" in Shakespeare's *Much Ado About Nothing* at the Brattle Theatre Shakespeare Festival in Cambridge, Massachusetts. Afterward, she joined the cast of *The Two Gentlemen of Verona* at Meisner's Neighborhood Playhouse. These productions were welcomed breaths of fresh air from sarongs and bows and arrows.

Sanford Meisner's technique emphasizes truthful and authentic performances. It is based on the belief that actors should fully immerse themselves in the present moment and respond truthfully to their surroundings and fellow actors. This approach encourages actors to let go of preconceived notions and rely on their instincts—something that greatly appealed to the very instinctually driven Susan.

The principles of Sanford Meisner's approach to acting were a much better fit to Susan's conventional take on her craft compared to Strasberg's method. Meisner espoused selfless authenticity and mindfulness, "living truthfully under imaginary circumstances." Under Meisner's direct training, Susan sharpened her characterization techniques in fully immersing herself within her characters' emotions and objectives. For Susan, this approach served as both a personally therapeutic process and excellent professional training. Susan connected with refining her character portrayal without the deep psychological exploration method acting requires. Her view was that acting offered a pseudo-tranquilizing escape from her pervasive psychological pain, and the method tried to remove that soothing quality altogether.

After reconnecting with the seasoning of urban theatre and regaining some of her self-confidence that she was in fact more than what the studio had given her credit for, she called former Universal-International recruiter, Al Mendelsohn, and asked for an agent. He took her to Peter Witt's office.

Witt looked from Susan to Al and back again in almost annoyed silence. "The way things are, I am awfully busy and not looking for new clients. It takes all my time properly to serve the ones I've got," Witt said casually from behind his desk. Susan quickly stood up to leave, "Thanks anyway," she said. Just before she reached the door, Witt said, "Hey, wait. Can you sing?"

From Susan's "yes," Witt phoned Robert Fryer, who happened to be producing a musical version of *Lost Horizon* called *Shangri-La*. With his cigarette smoke billowing over the desk, Susan's heart pounded with what the phone call could mean. "I've got this girl here, Bob, and the height is right, she's short, and the coloring is nice and she says she can sing, but who knows. If your lead isn't cast, you could hear her. Tomorrow? 2:00pm." Susan left Witt's office with a simple nod.

She was supposed to meet Witt at 1:55pm at Broadway's legendary Italian restaurant Sardi's. Nervous about the nearly "forced" appointment that Witt unenthusiastically arranged for her, Susan called Mendelsohn at noon to cancel. "I'm sorry Al, I just can't be there today. I forgot I promised to read with a guy at Meisner's." Mendelsohn blew a fuse on the other end of the line. "First, you didn't even thank Peter when we left yesterday. Now you want to blow the date?! You're crazy! You be there or don't *ever* call me again," he bellowed before a sharp slam of the phone.

Susan was at Sardi's at 1:55pm sharp, and Witt escorted her to the audition. She coolly approached the stage and sang. "[She] forthwith got the star role—by indifference, carelessness, casualness, and luck," columnist Whitney Bolton said. One newspaper even exaggerated that Susan merely "hummed" for her audition and still landed the role. Susan was cast as "Lo-Tsen" in the show, and on May 30, 1956, Susan Cabot made her Broadway debut—sort of.

But there is one that hasn't been done to death: it's the one about the girl who breaks every rule in the book and has Broadway thrust at her. It has just happened. Once. This girl is named Susan Cabot.

Before opening at the Winter Garden Theatre, there were supposedly loads of show revisions necessary under Robert Fryer and Lawrence Carr as the writers, and Albert Marre as director. Due to so many edits and reedits, there was a pre-opening run in Boston at the Shubert Theatre from which both Susan and leading man Lew Ayres eventually dropped out before it hit Broadway. Susan was replaced by Shirley Yamaguchi, and Ayres was replaced by Dennis King for Broadway's opening on June 13, 1956. The still troubled production only ran for twenty-one performances.

Return to Tinseltown

After the *Shangri-La* fiasco, Susan was naturally a little disillusioned with what New York had to offer her from that point. She joined other theatre guild efforts in New York productions, such as *Knickerbocker Holiday* with Will Geer later in 1956. She also toured outside the Northeastern circuit for a few stage productions, including *The Champagne Complex* in Myrtle Beach, South Carolina.

By 1957, Susan was done with New York once again and decided to give Hollywood another go. In making the decision to return to the West Coast, she felt steadier in her acting and singing ability and planned to take on Hollywood again—this time with even more perspective on the rules of the game. With age thirty just months away, she acknowledged a shift in priorities, however. While still driven, the ticking of her biological clock began to grow louder with the approach of thirty and drowned out the former hope of Milan: "Frankly, what I'd like the most in this world would be to have a *happy* home and a family."

But as any artist must do, Susan had to adjust the sails of her personal desires to correspond with the wind conditions, and when producer-director Roger Corman first saw Susan, the winds changed in a B-movie mania kind of direction.

Chapter Three
B-Movie Mania

"Life is like a B-movie. You don't want to leave in the middle of it, but you don't want to see it again."

— Ted Turner

By the Spring of 1957, Susan was back in Hollywood for round two. For a woman, taking Hollywood by storm at thirty years old was very different than doing so at twenty-four. Naturally her offerings, preferences, and priorities would be a little different after seven years of being "processed" through the entertainment industry on both the East and West coasts. In July of 1957, Susan became reacquainted with the small screen through her guest role on an episode of *Kraft Theatre*. She also had a role offer from director-producer Roger Corman, whom she had first met in New York before her second Hollywood try. Roger recalled their introduction in a 2000 *E!* interview:

> *I was doing some readings for an actress to play the wife of "Machine-Gun Kelly." From the beginning, the intensity, the power that she had, I knew almost as soon as she walked into the room that she was going to be the choice.*

Roger Corman

Known as "The King of Cult" or "King of the Bs" in some circles, Roger Corman is one of the most prolific film producer-directors in industry history. As a Detroit native, Roger grew up wanting to follow in his father's engineering footsteps until his Stanford University days, in which he developed an unignorable interest in film. Even though he graduated with an engineering degree, he found the industry wasn't where his passion lay after reportedly only three days on the job with US Electrical Motors. He instead got a job as a messenger at Twentieth Century Fox in their mail room and worked his way up to story analyst.

Under the G.I. Bill, Roger spent time in England, enrolled in Oxford University, followed by an extended tour of Europe, before he returned to the US and wrote his film script called *The House in the Sea*. He sold the script to Allied Artists, and they retitled the film *Highway Dragnet*. The 1953 film starred Richard Conte and Joan Bennett.

Even though Roger was technically the associate producer of the film, he was shocked by how his vision for the original script had been lost in screen adaptation. In vowing to produce his next script himself to avoid the degeneration of any artistic meaning, he set himself up for one of the most successful independent film careers in media history. Through his work with Allied Artists, American International Pictures, and major-player studios for a time, he produced and directed film after film with little to no budgets in remarkably short order. There is supposedly a well-known saying in Hollywood that Roger Corman could negotiate the production of a film on a pay phone, shoot the film in the booth, and finance it with the money in the change slot. Some of his better-known films include sci-fi *House of Usher* (1960) starring Vincent Price, *The Man with the X-Ray Eyes* (1963) starring Ray Milland, and *Frankenstein Unbound* (1990) starring John Hurt.

Roger has written, produced, directed, and performed in hundreds of films from his first in 1953 to his most recent as of 2023 at age ninety-seven, won countless awards, and has been an industry mentor to almost any big name you can think of. Among the most recognized of his mentees are Jack Nicholson, Robert De Niro, and Sandra Bullock. Roger is a filmmaking genius and industry legend who saw the great artistic benefit in running the show (quite literally) his own way. Roger's longstanding philosophy on filmmaking is, "Motion pictures are the art form of the 20th century, and one of the reasons is the fact that films are a slightly corrupted art form. They fit this century—they combine art and business!"

He is internationally recognized as a pioneer in "monster films," horror, sci-fi, the science of exploitation productions, and independent filmmaking. With his unwavering expertise in casting, when he invited Susan Cabot into his legacy back in 1957, it was something neither would regret.

Roger successfully recruited Susan for the rockabilly musical film, *Carnival Rock*, primarily because the lead female role of "Natalie Cook" finally gave her the opportunity to sing on screen. "Natalie" is the starlet of a carnival pier nightclub, and her boss "Christy" (played by David J. Stewart) romantically pursues her to the point of sheer madness when he learns she has become involved with "Stanley" (played by Brian G. Hutton), who wants to buy the nightclub from "Christy." Susan connected with the role in the obvious parallel of her own standing appointment as a nightclub singer, and she had fun filming as a part of Roger's stock company. Along with Susan's musical talent, the film features a number of pop music stars of the 1950s, including The Platters, David Houston, Bob Luman and His Shadows, and The Blockbusters.

With Roger's infamy for speedy production completion, *Carnival Rock* was the first of three Roger Corman films that featured Susan in the year 1957.

Carnival Rock was released in September, *Sorority Girl* in October, and *The Saga of the Viking Women and Their Voyage to the Waters of the Great Sea Serpent* was released in December.

Sorority Girl (1957) was another of Roger's films that featured Susan in the feminine lead. The film tells the story of neurotic college student, "Sabra Tanner," who belligerently clashes with nearly her entire university in her on-campus experience. Spoiled, willful, and conniving with major "mom issues" that become apparent as the plot progresses, "Sabra" increasingly resorts to violence and blackmail in maladaptively striving for love and affection until the film's grim conclusion.

In the opening scene of *Sorority Girl*, Susan's character "Sabra" is sleeping in her dorm and awakens screaming from a nightmare. Schoolmate

"Ellie" runs in upon hearing the wail from her room and infamously says, "That scream you let out sounded like you were being murdered." Thirty years later, that line would become hauntingly ironic in Susan's personal life (and death).

Because of Roger's genius for low-budget films with often low-budget mechanics, his productions were not without safety issues that sometimes triggered Susan's anxieties. She recalled a frightening incident that occurred while filming *The Saga of the Viking Women and Their Voyage to the Waters of the Great Sea Serpent* that contributed to her taking a Roger break for a few months.

Roger Corman's *The Saga of the Viking Women and Their Voyage to the Waters of the Great Sea Serpent* (1957) is a fantasy-adventure film that follows the seafaring journey of Viking women of Stannjold in the search for their missing Viking men. During their harrowing journey, they encounter a sea serpent that destroys their ship, leaving them stranded in the foreign land of Grimaults, where they are taken captive by the land's dictator, "Stark" (played by Richard Devon). While captive under Stark's rule, the women discover their beloved Viking men are also captives of Stark. Together, both groups overthrow their captors and return together to the land of Stannjold. Susan portrays fiery Viking woman, "Enger," who is among the most determined of the group. From its lengthy title to its special effects, the film is over-the-top-campy, but like many of Corman's 1950s works, it has become a cult classic. In a 1994 interview for *Sci Fi Entertainment*, Corman elaborated on the lengthy title chosen for the film:

> *The full title is* The Saga of the Viking Women and Their Voyage to the Waters of the Great Sea Serpent. *We couldn't figure out a way to put the title in two or three words, so I said let's go to the other extreme and give them the longest title they've ever seen and then use the greatest cliché in historical pictures at the time which is to open up on an engraved leather book, a hand comes in, opens the cover of the book, and there's the title of the picture.*

While shooting the scene in which the Viking women begin their sea journey in search of their missing male counterparts, the boat they are seen in met with catastrophe. Susan and the ten other female actresses who made up the band of Viking women were pulled out to sea by a crew boat in front outside of camera range. While the scene was shot, the tow boat's captain fell asleep and wasn't conscious enough to stop the boat. Despite the women's best efforts to wake him up with their shouting, their boat began rapidly taking on water. Susan was an avid swimmer and so was actress Abby Dalton, who played "Desir," but the others aboard were not.

The sinking group of faux-Vikings was finally able to catch the attention of others on the water, who sailed back toward shore to alert the crew of the vessel's predicament. Because of the choppy, rising waves at sea that day, Susan recalled that before help could reach them, they were forced to save themselves. The sinking boat finally moved close enough to the cliffs of the shore that they climbed the steep rocks to safety. They were all incredibly shaken from the incident, and Roger Corman got an earful from Susan afterward.

After *The Saga of the Viking Women and Their Voyage to the Waters of the Great Sea Serpent*, Susan took a Roger break and accepted a role in Joseph M. Newman's Western drama *Fort Massacre*, starring Joel McCrea and Forrest Tucker. She played yet another "Indian girl" role.

Joseph Newman's *Fort Massacre* follows a group of Union soldiers led by "Sergeant Vinson" (played by Joel McCrea) as they are ambushed by Apache warriors while on a mission to deliver a peace treaty. Like many Westerns of the era, the film explores themes of survival, loyalty, and the harsh realities of war. Susan portrays the description-only role of "Piute Girl."

Later in 1958, she went back to Roger for two more films that year: *War of the Satellites* and *Machine-Gun Kelly*. They may not have been Elizabeth Taylor roles Roger was offering her, but during that season of her life, Susan preferred campy B-movie mania to what Universal-International had in mind.

In the throes of the Cold War, the world witnessed the long-awaited first success in space exploration. "Sputnik," the world's first artificial satellite, was launched by the Soviet Union on October 4, 1957. Sputnik's groundbreaking blast off marked the beginning of the Space Age, as the satellite orbited the Earth for three months, transmitting radio signals back to eager, gravity-bound civilians across the globe. Its successful launch demonstrated the Soviet Union's technological prowess and sparked a space race between the United States and the Soviet Union. Sputnik had a tremendous impact on science, technology, and international relations from which further advancements in space exploration and satellite technology were made possible.

With Sputnik's launch on October 4, the race to conquer space had officially begun. The United States responded soon after with the launch of Explorer 1 on January 31, 1958. This intense rivalry between the two major geopolitical powers of the 1950s led to significant advancements in space technology (and beyond) in laying the foundation for future space exploration endeavors.

It all seems very straightforward to us now in the postmodern world, where space travel has become nearly as common as air travel, but in the 1950s, it was altogether different. Millions of civilians were skeptical of mystical endeavors beyond the stratosphere where gravity ceased to exist. There were loads of tall tales amid the uncertainties about what such experimental journeys could mean for the human race, especially since the Soviet Union traversed "the gulf of space" before the United States. From extraterrestrial invasions to satellite mechanical malfunctions that could zap planet Earth with one laser beam, many were overcome by hysterics. The 1950s weren't far removed from the mass hysteria caused by Orson Welles' *War of the Worlds* radio broadcasts of the 1930s, and when news of authentic space exploration broke, recollections of H.G. Wells' (1897) text flooded back through Byron Haskin's on-screen adaptation of Wells' sci-fi classic in 1953:

Yet across the gulf of space, minds that are to our minds as ours are to those of the beasts that perish, intellects vast and cool and unsympathetic, regarded this earth with envious eyes, and slowly and surely drew their plans against us.

Naturally, Hollywood capitalized on the masses' response to such a phenomenon in their production efforts, which initiated a new era of sci-fi films. Producers and directors like Don Siegel (*Invasion of the Body Snatchers*) and Jack Arnold (*It Came from Outer Space*), who were accomplished in horror, dramatized the dichotomy of thrills and fears of the 1950s' audiences. Roger Corman joined the trend with Irving Block's *War of the Satellites*.

In a 2019 *Variety* interview, Roger recalled how the idea of *War of the Satellites* was first conceived:

I remember when the first Sputnik went up, I heard about it that night. At nine o'clock the next morning, I was in Steve Broidy's office at Allied Artists. And I said, 'Steve, if you can give me $80,000, I will have a picture about satellites ready to go into the theaters in 90 days.' And then he said, 'What's the story?' And I said, 'I have no idea, but I will have the picture ready.' And he said, 'Done.' And he gave me the money. And so we went off and made War of the Satellites.

The film tells the story of an invisible entity that wages war against planet Earth when the United Nations fails to heed warnings during attempts to assemble the first space satellite. Susan was cast as lead female scientist "Sybil Carrington" opposite Dick Miller as "Dave Boyer," lead male scientist. On a $70,000 budget, the film only took eight weeks to shoot. Upon its release it was met with solid reception, and has been one of Roger's hundreds to go down as a cult classic B-movie.

Susan made the leap from astrophysicist to gun moll for her role in Roger's next 1958 production: *Machine-Gun Kelly*. The pseudo-biographical film delves into the life and career of notorious Prohibition gangster, George "Machine-Gun" Kelly. From the film's intense action sequences to unexpected tender moments of human connection, Roger gives audiences an alternative perspective of the lawless legacy of "Machine-Gun Kelly." Stereotyped tough-guy Charles Bronson portrays the infamous Kelly, and Susan portrays his partner-in-crime turned love interest, "Flo Becker." *Machine-Gun Kelly* is considered one of the most serious dramatic productions of Roger Corman's twentieth-century film work.

With her knack for roles of great intensity, Susan was often cast in villainous roles within Roger's films. *Sorority Girl* (1957), *The Saga of the Viking Women and Their Voyage to the Waters of the Great Sea Serpent* (1957), and *Machine-Gun Kelly* (1958) showcased some of her most fervid on-screen work in portraying calculating, maniacal leading women. Susan told film historian Tom Weaver of her experience in playing those types of roles:

> *I loved it from the standpoint of their being a challenge, but it was very hard for me to play an unfeeling character—to do or say something cruel to another person, not feeling it in my bones or in my heart, and know that that other person is suffering. I've been victimized by people like that, and it hurts.*

Surrender — Hell!

Susan did an episode on *Have Gun — Will Travel* in 1958 and accidentally gave Richard Boone a lifetime scar when she swung her rifle a little too enthusiastically, and it flew out of her hand. "I've played baseball," Susan told Leonard Lyons. "I'm a good hitter. I swung the rifle, thinking I could hold it back in time, as if for a bunt. Instead, I hit him for a triple," she blushed.

That Spring, she began filming for a role in John Barnwell's film: *Surrender — Hell!* Barnwell wrote and directed the Allied Artists production starring Keith Andes and Susan Cabot as his leading lady—well, sort of.

Surrender — Hell! is a war drama based on the memoir of WWII commander, Lt. Donald D. Blackburn, in his refusal to surrender to the Japanese or the treacherous conditions of the island of Luzon. In his survival efforts, Blackburn leads a group of local natives in a fight against the Japanese invasion. Susan plays the role of the beautiful local village girl "Delia

Guerrero" who helps Blackburn in his militant plight in the first half of the film.

In authentic form, the film was actually shot in the jungles of the Philippines, and much of the cast and crew (especially Susan) dealt with many challenges that come with the region, like the unrelenting jungle humidity, mosquitoes by the swarms, rough and unpredictable terrain, and tented accommodations with few luxuries. With little to no safeguards in place to protect the cast and crew from the rainforest's natural inhabitants such as the crocodiles, snakes, and leeches, they were all on high alert while filming. Supposedly, the crew put chemicals into some of the pools to kill off the majority of the leeches, but of course, no one can tame a whole jungle.

One account Susan recalled in an interview with Marjory Adams with *The Boston Globe* gives a glimpse into the conditions. She and leading man Keith Andes went for a swim in a small, seemingly safe lagoon. Neither knew until a few minutes into their "swim" that the water was full of leeches that survived the chemical raid. Susan quickly swam to shore and scrambled to the "safety" of the dry bank. A G.I. appearing in the film invasively approached her with a cigarette and commanded her to stand still. With no words, he burned three leeches off her back with his cigarette. The leeches she couldn't see had been clinging to her wet skin. That was reportedly only one of the many jungle horrors that contributed to Susan's desertion of the project. She weighed only eighty-three pounds when she boarded the plane home to Los Angeles.

Personal safety was Susan's paramount priority given the arduous trajectory of her childhood and young adult life. She was a constant flight risk because if she perceived a threat of any kind, she was out, no questions asked. This self-preservation strategy may have helped her avoid feeling revictimized in adulthood, but it did little to establish a reputation for reliability as an actress.

In that production, perhaps much like Broadway's *Shangri-La*, there was too much discomfort of some kind or other and she didn't feel safe. When her complaints went largely unheard, she left mid-production. It is conspicuously noticeable in the film that her leading role disappears halfway through. Barnwell patched the scripting and added another female character to the storyline as a redemptive effort in smoothing over her ghosting the production. The native Philippine actress, Paraluman, played the role of "Pilar" who becomes Lt. Blackburn's love interest and helpmate in his eventual victory.

I Mobster

Once back in Los Angeles, safe from the humidity and jungle discomfort, Susan picked back up where she left off in her career and social engagements. In July of 1958, Roger was filming the crime drama *I Mobster* starring Steve Cochran and Lita Milan. While it's no oddity for producers and directors to have on-set trouble with their principal actors, Roger and the twenty-four-year-old Lita had more than just the standard artistic differences on the set of this film. The trouble caused Roger to offer Susan Lita's lead role as "Teresa Porter," the lady friend of gang lord, "Joe Sante" (played by Steve Cochran).

The "mysterious lady in red" became a hot topic in many newspapers in the Summer of 1958 when a beautiful, unnamed woman was "kidnapped" by a yacht in San Pedro on July 15, 1958. The vessel was later identified as *Angelita*, the yacht of Dominican playboy General Rafael "Ramfis" Trujillo, Jr. Just before Roger began shooting on location for *I Mobster*, his leading lady vanished coincidentally at the same time the reports of "the lady in red" circulated.

Trujillo's four-masted yacht was spotted creeping along the dock line until her crew encountered the "lady in red" waiting on the boardwalk. While there are several contradictory accounts, many reported the "lady in red" was physically forced to board the yacht against her will. After she boarded, she managed to break free of her captors and run down the gangplank away from the vessel, when two men pursued her and once again forcibly carried her back inside the 350-foot ship, after which it sped away.

A few days later, the "lady in red" was identified as "fiery Hollywood starlet" Lita Milan when she phoned Roger from San Diego to ask if he would consider postponing filming until she returned. Through phone static, he managed to determine she was in no immediate danger, but had been coerced into vacationing with the charming Ramfis so he could "properly" ask for her hand in marriage.

Having been left in the lurch by his leading lady, Roger was in no mood to postpone. Instead, he proceeded with filming after tagging Susan Cabot for Lita's role. Susan readily accepted, but after only a few days of filming, Lita returned from her mysterious rendezvous and replaced her replacement. Susan was ousted, and Lita completed the film as "Teresa."

I Mobster was Lita's last film. She later married Ramfis in 1960. He died in 1969 of pneumonia. Ironically, Lita said in a 2013 interview that her marriage to Ramfis was "a gallant kidnapping. He was a dark prince on a white horse. But at the same time, it was my mistake because I could have gone much further as an actress."

The King

Despite her occasional breaks from Hollywood, Susan remained connected with friends and LA nightlife that often afforded elaborate dinner parties, limousines, and dashing suitors. In April of 1959, Susan began seeing a Middle Eastern dignitary and made all the papers with their unusual romance. King Hussein of Jordan and B-movie queen Susan Cabot were an unlikely pair, playing on all columns' speculations of how they became acquainted and what the true nature of their relationship was. On January 9, 2018, *only* fifty-nine years later, the *New York Post* cleared things up with a declassified government memo. Susan was propositioned by the CIA to be an escort for King Hussein. Upon receiving the memo, she promptly refused such an assignment. Ironically, she ended up falling for the King on her own terms with no help from the CIA.

The establishment of the Central Intelligence Agency (CIA) in 1947 marked a significant turning point in American history. Created under the National Security Act, the CIA was tasked with gathering and analyzing intelligence to protect national security interests following World War II. The war had exposed many weaknesses in America's intelligence infrastructure, leading policymakers to recognize the importance of a singularly dedicated agency. Further, growing tensions with the Soviet Union during the Cold War necessitated an organization capable of monitoring for communist threats through covert operations and espionage.

The establishment of the CIA represented a response to post-war challenges and an evolution in American foreign policy. While it has been subject to criticism over some of its methods and actions since it was instituted, there is no denying its enduring impact on the United States' national security efforts and history overall. But what does the CIA have to do with matchmaking?

In an effort to maintain congenial international relations, the CIA would often assist foreign dignitaries in their arrangements when planning a visit to the United States. Occasionally these dignitaries, who were often men, would request the companionship of a beautiful and governmentally vetted female for their American tour. The CIA used its intimate knowledge of civilian profiles to misogynistically match these dignitaries with the perfect escort. Hollywood starlets made great candidates according to the CIA, and they compiled binders of female profiles from which to choose. For King Hussein's 1959 American tour, they somehow thought the *Jewish* beauty Susan Cabot would make a perfect match for the *Muslim* royal dignitary.

The King, Revisited

According to the *New York Post*, in late 1958, King Hussein of Jordan was planning his first visit to Los Angeles, California. He was only twenty-four years old, but in inheriting the imperial throne of Jordan and rulership of the West Bank as a teenager, he was a foreign dignitary that the United States government longed to appease in his American tour. His staff coordinated with the CIA in preparation for his visit to secure a beautiful (and well-vetted) American woman to be his Los Angeles escort in April of 1959.

The CIA selected Susan from a registry of attractive, notable women who might accompany the recently divorced King during his California stay. In the government's misogynistic matchmaking efforts, they penned a proposal to Susan detailing the "assignment," which required her to graciously represent her country in attending a high-profile party with King Hussein. In the spirit of patriotism and hospitality, the proposal also required her "to go to bed with him afterward." Susan vehemently declined that particular term of the proposal but attended the party anyway.

She was busy filming *The Wasp Woman* in time for its Halloween release that year, but one party couldn't hurt, especially when it was the soiree of oil tycoon Edwin Pauley in Southern California. Susan and the King met at the party organically. He was everything his title implied: handsome, intelligent, debonair, and a bit irresistible as the night inched on. He, of course, found Susan to be of ethereal quality with her dark hair and eyes, elegant frame, and delicate temperament.

The two fenced all evening with small-talk, soft glances, and mutual wonderment. A simple kiss ended the evening, much to the chagrin of the King *and* the CIA, but a few days later Susan received another proposition. He wanted her to also accompany him during his New York visit. The CIA took out a room for Susan under a pseudonym at the Hotel Barclay, and the two took on New York City in grandeur. After several winsome dates during the King's stay, the couple eventually fulfilled the CIA's "requirements" and went to bed together on their own non-governmental terms. He and Susan stayed in contact after his return to Jordan, but both knew there was no viable future for any long-term romance. After all, he was the ruler of a Middle Eastern nation and she a mere American civilian, though the greatest complication existed in the spiritual contrast of his Muslim heritage to her Jewish one. The two discreetly continued contact with periodic interludes upon the King's subsequent visits to America, though later it was revealed they were more like good buddies than star-crossed lovers. Susan said, "I met him, that's all. But the experts put some rumors together, and suddenly I was the love of his life." Susan was a self-reported introvert and preferred to keep her private life private, giving mere clues to the press. She didn't discuss details of their relationship and neither did he. Naturally, the press and fans relished in the play on words: "King Hussein and the Queen Wasp."

When she was asked whether she would like to see King Hussein again after their first publicized date, she answered carefully: "I think he has too many worries in his country without getting involved with any one person. He's harassed on all sides, even by his neighbors. He's a very sensitive person and I respect him." Susan said she referred to the King as "Your Majesty" while they rendezvoused on the town, but over dinner and under sheets, he was just "Sam."

Hussein bin Talal was born on November 14, 1935, in Amman. He is considered the longest-serving monarch in Jordan's modern history. He ascended to the throne at seventeen, following the assassination of his grandfather, King Abdullah I, and his father King Talal's abdication in 1952. Throughout his 46-year reign, King Hussein played a significant role in shaping Jordan's domestic and foreign policies, though his legacy has drawn both accolades and criticism. Avi Shlaim, in the 2009 biography of Hussein *Lion of Judah*, says,

> *Hussein's supporters see him as a man who consistently pursued a strategy of peace and ultimately succeeded in bridging the historic gulf by concluding a peace treaty with Israel. His critics take a radically different view of his legacy of accommodation with Israel, seeing it as a surrender and a betrayal of the Palestinians.*

For his supporters, Hussein was and is widely regarded as a unifying figure in his tireless work to maintain stability and peace in the region. "I will never work merely to make a reputation for myself, to be popular for appearances rather than for what I am. My task is to lead my country through service," Hussein said.

His critics, however, argued that much of Hussein's reign lacked transparency, accountability, and political freedom in his country, especially with regard to human rights issues. As an artful diplomat, however, his regent cabinet espoused progressive policies in the tedious relations with Arab nations, Palestine, Israel, and the West.

King Hussein's rule wasn't without imperfections, but generally his progressive vision for his country was carried out to a revolutionary tune that had not been heard before. His push for peace through progressive ideals was evidenced in his commitment to social and economic development, however unconventional those ideals may have been to some. His forward efforts to promote dialogue and understanding among different religious and ethnic groups is also a distinct characteristic of his reign that wasn't particularly of conventional practice in the late twentieth century. He was also a champion of women and women's issues within the context of Islam:

> *I am totally against the idea that a Muslim woman should not have the same opportunities as a Muslim man to learn, to open up, to work, help shape the future. To close Islam down to a sexist approach is totally intolerable and ridiculous.*

His dedication to peace was evident in his role as a mediator in various regional conflicts, including the Camp David Accords in 1978. King Hussein's reign came to an end on February 7, 1999, when he passed away after a long battle with cancer. Hussein had received his final round of chemotherapy at the Mayo Clinic in Rochester, Minnesota, the week before his death upon returning home to Jordan. His son, King Abdullah, succeeded the throne, but Hussein's legacy as a visionary leader and an advocate of peace endures.

King Hussein was married four times and fathered eleven children, though many believe that number may be one higher if the rumors are true that he is the biological father of Susan's only child: Timothy Scott Roman.

Wasp Woman

At the end of Spring 1959, Susan was planning to leave for Nairobi to star in a new Tarzan film for CinemaScope, but it fell through before takeoff. In the Summer of 1959, she began filming for the role that became her most infamous: "Janice Starlin" in *The Wasp Woman*. The B-movie features many of Roger's stock company, including Susan in the lead with Anthony Eisley (also billed as Fred Eisley) and Barboura Morris in support. In Hitchcock fashion, Roger himself also cameoed in this film.

As president of a cosmetics corporation overly concerned with youthful looks, "Janice Starlin" experiments with a youth serum developed from the extract of wasps. The serum turns back time for "Janice" with the hope of also doing so for her customers, but the entire corporation soon learns that though the serum technically works, it comes with a host of deadly side effects. *Wasp Woman* offered Susan a trio of roles in playing the older "Janice" at the beginning of the film in her pre-injection state, younger "Janice" in the middle of the film after being injected with the serum, and the "lusting Queen Wasp" at the conclusion. Susan told Tom Weaver in a 1985 interview:

> *That was a lot of fun and a real challenge. In that film I played Janice Starlin, a character who, through injections of wasp enzymes, goes from a woman of forty to a woman of twenty-two. I had to play two roles differently. Older people usually move and speak more slowly, and I just used a slower pace, a more considered way of thinking for the 'old' Janice. Acting spontaneously, full of life, doing things off the top -- that was how I played the 'young' Janice. Since I'm small -- I'm 5'2" -- another challenge was figuring out a way to attack 6'4" men and make it look credible. The only way I felt I could convincingly down a bigger person was through swiftness -- by coming at them so fast, like a bolt of lightning, and staying right on target. It worked.*

Wasp Woman, known originally as *Insect Woman*, was filmed in just two weeks on a budget of $50,000. Susan did all of her own stunt work in the film, which was at times risky and not always without injury. Susan recalled the filming for the climax that was to be done in one shot. During the fight scene in the lab with Anthony Eisley, someone used a real bottle filled with water instead of a "breakaway" bottle, so when it hit Susan, she said to Tom Weaver, "...It hit like a rock. I thought my lower teeth came up through my nose. When you saw me hiding my face in that shot, it was because I was hurt very badly. But I continued to go through the scene!"

When a crew member poured liquid smoke into Susan's costumed antennae, he inadvertently poured too much. She said the mask immediately filled with billows of smoke, causing her to crash through the window. As she fell through the glass, she began choking on the chemical inside. The low-budget wasp mask had no breathability except for two tiny nostrils. The mask had been glued to her face, and when it filled up with smoke, she began "clawing and scratching" until someone finally realized she was in trouble. Crew members doused her with water, and she finally tore free of the mask, taking some of her skin with it.

Susan also said Roger insisted on showing audiences clear shots of "blood" that would drain from victims' necks after she bit them. Luckily, he settled for Hershey's chocolate in lieu of the real thing, though with his reputation for saving dimes on productions, many wondered why he splurged for the Hershey's when real blood was virtually free.

The Wasp Woman debuted in theatres on October 30, 1959, as a double feature along with Monte Hellman's *Beast from Haunted Cave*. Neither film was a box office smash, but Susan received positive reviews from many papers nationwide. Journalist Charles Stinson with *The Los Angeles Times* said, "Slim, intense brunette [sic] Susan Cabot, who always impresses, does excellently nuanced work as the neurotic lady with the worries and the wasps."

Science experiments gone wrong is always a thematic interest to movielovers, and with Corman's flair for the outrageous, *Wasp Woman* was a "hit" by sci-fi fan standards. The film accumulated a cult following in the years after its release and in 1995, director Jim Wynorski remade the classic for a TV movie starring Jennifer Rubin, Doug Wert, and Daniel J. Travanti. The original *Wasp Woman* was Susan's last film. In her Hollywood stint, she began on the silver screen with William Berke as an island girl at twenty-four and ended with Roger Corman as "Wasp Woman" at thirty-two.

Chapter Four
Timothy Scott Roman:
A Study in Statistics

"Most people use statistics like a drunk man uses a lamppost; more for support than illumination."

— Andrew Lang

In April of 1959, not long after meeting King Hussein, Susan flew back to New York for another Hollywood hiatus for the stage. She reportedly had an audition scheduled for a Broadway musical. Coincidentally, the King just happened to be travelling to New York too, as another stop on his American tour after taking a stopover in Palm Springs, where Susan also happened to be.

Susan had an engagement to star in *The Golden Fleecing* opposite Tom Poston under Abe Burrows' direction. The show opened at the Wilbur Theatre in Boston in September of 1959 and was headed for Broadway. Unfortunately, Susan was eventually replaced by the younger Suzanne Pleshette in the role of "Julie."

Susan kept up appearances in Manhattan's high society with the likes of Ludlow Stevens and Arthur "Dick" Cowan at Latin Quarter and El Morocco. Though a self-reported "hermit" at heart, Susan had just as many friends in New York as she did in Los Angeles, so she suffered no social deprivation with her back-and-forth pace between the two cities. No matter which "home" she retreated to, she always maintained close contact with girlfriends Kathleen Hughes, Mamie Van Doren, and Lori Nelson.

She also had an "analyst" in each city, either of whom she could phone at nearly any hour for auditory championing or guidance. While she casually dated (and for a while seriously dated actor Sydney Pollock), she was "still hoping [for marriage] because I would like to have loads of children. I love my work but when it is done, I want to go home quietly and read, paint, or sing."

From early 1959 through 1966, Susan's career was a blur of television and stage. She occasionally appeared on *Ellery Queen*, *Pantomime Quiz*, and television's adaptation of Irna Phillip's soap *Brighter Day* while also devoting her talents to regional theatre in off-Broadway productions.

After all, Susan couldn't do just one thing. She had to have at least two art forms to vacillate between, and for the 1960s, television and stage fit better than television and B-movies. She said in an interview with journalist Don Royal:

> *Picture after picture that I wasn't particularly proud of making. But I have tried in every film to get some kind of meaning out of my part. So, the time wasn't entirely wasted. And I did earn some money. But now I'm back in New York, taking singing lessons and looking for the kind of parts I should have tried for years ago. I haven't given up on opera, but I'm thirty, and I have the feeling that musical comedy is as close as I'll get. I've reached the stage where I understand myself a little bit. Now I want to fulfill myself. I know I haven't realized my potential at all. I've got this little apartment now that's a mess, but it's wonderful for me. I'm sculpting and painting and getting reacquainted with New York. I'm not bitter about Hollywood, but it's time for me to get a move on. Life is very exciting if you work at it.*

Susan suffered from a string of health issues in the early 1960s, which interfered with her work and social life. In November 1962, while starring in the off-Broadway production *Intimate Relations*, Susan became ill halfway through the first act. She "complained of sharp stomach pains while standing backstage waiting to return to her role during the first act." She was rushed to a nearby hospital and underwent an emergency appendectomy while her understudy, Sally Schinerhern, took over in her place.

In her recovery, she began seriously dating actor Christopher "Chris" Jones. After they broke their relationship off, he went on to marry actress Susan Strasberg, daughter of Lee Strasberg, who developed the method acting for which Susan had such great professional disdain. Jones later said in an interview about his tryst with Susan: "We'd only been together three weeks, then I just sort of disappeared."

Christopher Jones was an enigmatic actor who rose to fame in the 1960s with his brooding good looks and intense performances. Born William Franklin Jones on August 18, 1941, in Jackson, Tennessee, he first gained attention in his role as the troubled teenager turned revolutionary in Barry Shear's *Wild in the Streets* (1968). His performance was praised for its raw intensity and emotional depth, earning him critical acclaim and the 1968 winner of the Golden Laurel for "Male New Face."

However, despite his promising start, Jones wrestled with many personal demons that hindered his career. He battled drug addiction and suffered from mental health issues that ultimately led to his untimely retirement from acting after his last film, David Lean's *Ryan's Daughter* (1970).

Despite leaving Hollywood behind at the young age of twenty-nine for a quieter life with his family, Chris Jones remains an intriguing figure in film history. His talent and potential were undeniable, leaving audiences wondering what could have been if not for his myriad personal struggles. Chris was married three times and fathered seven children, though many believe that number may be one higher if the rumors are true that he is the biological father of Susan's only child: Timothy Scott Roman.

***

Still dreaming of marriage and a happy family, she reportedly moved to London for a time after New York and married a British diplomat, which may have been a red herring away from how she truly spent her mid-1960s.

Susan still dreamed of getting remarried and starting a family with the "loads of children" she longed for, and on January 27, 1964, she began to realize that dream when her son Timothy "Tim" Scott Wingate was born.

The name "Timothy" is of Greek origin, and it means "he who honors God."

It was a Loretta Young and Clark Gable story.

Well-known actress suddenly disappears from the public eye for a time, comes back with a baby, blames the milkman, the school zone guy, the parking lot attendant…anybody but the real sperm donor.

In Washington, D.C., on January 27, 1964, thirty-seven-year-old Susan gave birth to her only child: Timothy "Tim" Scott Wingate. It was reportedly a very difficult birth for them both. She had emergency surgery to correct a twisted intestine, and doctors found it necessary to do a cesarean section during the initial operation. She went under anesthesia pregnant for what was supposed to be a routine repair and woke up to a very premature baby in an oxygen tent next to her bed. A barely two-pound Tim suffered a number of complications as a result of his prematurity and difficult birth, including an underdeveloped respiratory system, periodic seizures, hypoglycemia, and brain damage. He spent four months in what we now know as the Neonatal Intensive Care Unit (NICU) in Washington, D.C. When he was stable enough to be discharged, Susan took Tim "home" to her aunt's house, not far from the hospital. She and her mother, Muriel, had reconnected by the time Tim was born, and Susan let her birth family baby the fledgling little Tim as they had done to her years before the Shapiro house erupted scattering Philip, Muriel, and Harriet to the ends of the earth for decades.

Historically, premature birth was a phenomenon largely associated with negative outcomes or death, until the late twentieth century, when advancements in obstetrics and pediatrics began to change the trajectories for infants in neonatal care. The establishment of specialized neonatal units in hospitals marked a turning point in medicine, largely brought about by the early birth of Patrick Bouvier Kennedy, the son of President Kennedy and First Lady. GBH reporter Gabrielle Emanuel (2021) says:

Many people trace the improvements in preemie care back to late fall 1963. That's when the world held its breath for 39 hours after First Lady Jackie Kennedy gave birth to a son five and a half weeks early. He was airlifted from Cape Cod to Boston and doctors desperately tried to save him, but they failed. Patrick Bouvier Kennedy's short life had a big impact. There was suddenly an investment in preemie research, an infusion of resources, a sense of urgency. Soon, NICUs were proliferating. And it wasn't long before a medical specialty was created to care for preemies and other newborns.

In the early twentieth century, incubators were introduced as a means to provide a controlled environment for premature infants. These devices helped regulate temperature, humidity, and oxygen levels, greatly enhancing their chances of survival. Additionally, breakthroughs in nutrition and infection control further improved outcomes for premature babies.

The mid-twentieth century witnessed significant advancements with the introduction of mechanical ventilation techniques to support respiratory function in preterm infants. This innovation revolutionized neonatal care by allowing doctors to manage respiratory distress more effectively.

Today, one in ten babies is born prematurely. Luckily, NICUs are now equipped with state-of-the-art technology and staffed by highly skilled healthcare professionals who specialize in caring for premature babies. Continuous monitoring systems, advanced imaging techniques, and life-saving medications have become standard practice and have flipped the mortality rates from 95% chance of death with a 5% chance of survival to 5% chance of death with a 95% chance of survival.

Tim was one of millions of premature babies born in the 1960s, but he was one of only a handful to beat the odds of the 95% mortality risk. The approach to neonatal care was very different in 1964 compared to today throwing Susan as a single new mother into a tormenting experience: "In this era, hospitals had the mindset that only doctors and nurses should care for the baby until he or she was ready to come home," Christel Cornell, with the NICU at Children's Hospital of Illinois said.

Susan and Tim both used much of 1964 to stabilize. Because Susan's intestinal operation and C-section virtually took place at the same time, she had a grueling "double" recovery process that required her to learn to walk again. Susan told columnist Dorothy Manners Haskell, "I couldn't walk for eight months following the birth of Scott. Both the baby and I barely made it…"

Susan was discharged from recovery within a week of Tim's birth, but Tim remained in the care of strangers for his first four months with little contact with the mother who birthed him. When she was strong enough to be wheeled to the neonatal unit, occasionally, a sympathetic charge nurse would allow Susan to sneak a stroke to Tim's little red face or hand, but most of her visits consisted only of a few quick peeks through his oxygen tent panel. With the wires and tubes and constant shooing of the staff, Susan felt a terrible emptiness. Her body hadn't been ready to naturally deliver Tim when he was taken by cesarean while she lay unconscious on the operating table. As she physically endured severe pain in recovery, the psychological pain of it all may have been worse. In the weeks and months following Tim's birth, she faced a tremendous amount of disenfranchised grief in having a baby too soon that she couldn't even hold or kiss until medical experts permitted her to. The physical and emotional trauma, coupled with the statistically grim outlook for Tim, made 1964 one of the most devilish seasons in Susan's life.

Whatever time mother and son had been separated by his neonatal care, she made up for in constant hugs, kisses, and presence once he was discharged. By the Spring of 1966, Susan was ready to break away from her temporary Washington, D.C., stopover and prepared to take Tim back to Los Angeles to raise him. In June of that year, Susan and two-year-old Tim settled as California residents. As a devoted single mother, Susan was proud and protective of little Tim, following the doctor's recommendations to the letter, but where, and more specifically, *who* was his father?

Because of their well-publicized romance, many speculated King Hussein was, in fact, Tim's father. This speculation may have also been influenced by the "mysterious" and "foreign" themes related to her on-screen work in Kurt Neumann's film *Son of Ali Baba* (1952). Years later, newspapers reported $1,500 monthly deposits from a trust fund in Jordan had been made into Susan's bank account, and many believed that solidified the King's fatherhood of Tim. Michael later denied those reports of Susan being regularly supported by King Hussein. Chris Jones, Marlon Brando, Rock Hudson, and even Cyril Raymond were also fingered as Tim's father, but Susan seemed impervious to public conjecture. She adored Tim and believed her love was strong enough to provide both a mother and a father's nurturing to him.

Though whatever romance between Susan and Hussein went largely unrequited in terms of wedding bells, the King reportedly financially supported Susan for years after their initial meeting. For a time, he did shower her with expensive gifts of jewelry and furs, occasional monetary gifts, and luxury cars such as her Bentley and Mercedes-Benz that had the custom-made license plate "S000Z." Susan Cabot sported the finest dresses Bullock's offered.

There were, of course, prodigious amounts of gossip about how Susan could afford such things (even in maintenance if they were originally gifts), but Susan was frugal and invested her money in real estate, vintage car flipping, and the stock market. Part of her luxurious lifestyle may have been initially funded by Jordan's throne, but Susan earned her own money as an acting instructor, her occasional television roles, and royalties from the Screen Actors Guild. She managed her collective funds well, never giving "Sam" reason to resent his generous gifts.

Susan's second husband, Michael Roman, later said Susan and "Sam" would call each other for friendly chats. She never specifically discussed the relationship with him, but Michael said "Sam" would always remember Susan's birthday with packages, as well as Tim's and Susan's mother, Muriel's. Michael told Tom Weaver, "It was almost like a brother-sister relationship, they really hit it off, aside from the romance that they had many years before. They just had a good friendship."

Susan and Tim settled in Encino, California. Susan bought an 11,000 square foot showplace on Charmion Lane about fifteen minutes West of central Los Angeles. The newly built mansion had six bedrooms, ten baths, vaulted ceilings, and marble floors with luxurious amenities including a "floating staircase," two fireplaces, a sauna, library, and three-car garage. Inside one of Encino's most exclusive neighborhoods, the house was a white brick hilltop complete with maid quarters and panoramic view of the San Fernando Valley. Susan paid roughly $1,552,575 for the Charmion Lane home in the early 1970s.

Just Trust Us

Tim was an adorable little blonde boy who, much like his mother, was petite and appeared much younger than his age. While Tim remarkably beat the odds of the 95% mortality rate for preterm infants in the 1960s, his survival trajectory was uphill every inch of the way. He generally met his basic developmental milestones despite doctors' initial prophecies, but he essentially just *never* seemed to grow, no matter how much Susan supplemented his bottles and food with caloric boosters according to the doctor's recommendations. Even as a small child, Tim perhaps had more behavioral difficulties than his peers and was extremely attached to Susan. After her death, many were sure his overattachment to her was due to her alleged "neurotic" helicoptering, though the absence of a father-figure may have also partly been to blame, as Susan was his primary (and for his first four years, his *only*) caregiver.

Of course, it stands to reason someone, like Susan, with little to no consistent nurturing themselves would either be prone to reenacting their own neglect or over nurturing a child of their own, especially a child with severe physical and mental challenges. Susan chose the overcompensation of over nurturing; she pampered and coddled little Tim, keeping him thoroughly scrubbed and dressed in the finest children's clothing available on the West Coast. He had the latest toys, haircuts, and most elaborate birthday parties in Los Angeles. Spoiled though he may have been, Susan wanted him to have some type of "normalcy," though she may not have known quite how to give that to him. Though cautious about others watching him without her present when he was a baby, Susan recognized the importance of Tim's independence, at least to the extent that she enrolled him in preschool before he started in public school at age five.

With Tim's litany of medical conditions partly due to his extreme prematurity and partly due to some noted genetic abnormalities, he spent much of his early years in and out of specialist appointments and in-patient hospital stays. In the late 1960s, prematurity and its implications for healthy growth was still a bit mysterious and very much "treated" from a trial-and-error perspective by medical professionals. Aside from Tim's behavioral problems, the largest glaring issue was his lack of growth. When he was five, he reportedly had the bone structure and overall body weight of a two-year-old.

Susan was worn to fatigue with the constant regimen of adding nutrient powders to his baby food to increase his caloric intake, encouraging specific foods and meal timing to capitalize on optimal metabolization, and still the scale remained the same. For months and months, Susan sweated over every pound, meal, and pediatrician appointment. Tim simply would not grow.

At first, Susan blamed normal genetics for his small stature, because she, after all, had always been petite, but as he aged, it became clear something more serious was at play. Though the condition of dwarfism has always been a part of the human race, the medical study of the condition wasn't particularly robust in the United States in 1969.

There are categorically dozens of manifestations of dwarfism that hint at causation, but for Tim, his medical team diagnosed him with pituitary dwarfism. His condition was related to growth hormone deficiency. His pituitary gland made insufficient amounts of the hormones necessary to encourage healthy growth, leaving him with a shorter-than-average stature, but normal body proportions. The category of dwarfism condition that is most recognized is achondroplasia, which makes up about 70% of overall cases. Achondroplasia generally has the signature manifestation of disproportionate limb size in relation to overall body mass. Tim did not have this type of dwarfism; therefore, he appeared small and much younger than his age, but did not exhibit the more recognized manifestations of what many associate with a "dwarfism" diagnosis.

Pituitary dwarfism can be genetic but may also have causes that are related to early-childhood factors, such as an injury to the pituitary gland, or certain syndromes that do not always show up in utero or even in the first few years of life, especially not in 1969. It is unclear what "caused" Tim's condition, though it likely was due to genetic particulars, or perhaps related to his traumatic and critically early birth. Though causation is often impossible to tease out, whatever the cause of Tim's poorly functioning pituitary gland, Susan was interested in the recommendations of his medical team in helping him overcome the ill effects of such a diagnosis.

As a single mother who was virtually Tim's only advocate for most of his life, Susan had little choice but to cling to the white coats' recommendations. She diligently, and perhaps at times naively, followed their suggestions to the letter. Whether projected by patients, cultivated by physicians themselves, or a bit of both, for much of the twentieth century, a god-complex pervasively existed within the medical community that left only a slim margin for true advocacy on the part of parents. Susan was continually at the mercy of Tim's next referral, and whatever the next opinion of his care was, she religiously adjusted accordingly.

Biologically, Tim was an anomaly from the beginning. Doctors did not expect him to survive, and he did, so teasing out the residuals of his complicated medical history was dicey. In addition to his prematurity and enduring physical underdevelopment, Tim continued to suffer from periodic seizures and hypoglycemia well into his elementary school years. The diagnosis of dwarfism added to his brimming file yet another unexpected dimension with few treatment options.

Some shockumentaries and commentaries on Susan and Tim have suggested that she manically campaigned for Tim to have "magic potion" injections in order to make him grow. One radical source even suggested she paid a private "mad scientist" to formulate such a concoction. Those erroneous claims fail to consider the medical model of the 1960s and 1970s in the United States. Medical professionals had *great* authority in that era. Today, in the 2020s, in the United States, we find ourselves more in a "medical consumerism marketplace," where we have the liberation as patients to freely "get second opinions," often do our own research, and almost "partner" with our medical experts in self-advocacy to a degree that was unheard of in the 1960s and 1970s. We certainly do not "doctor" ourselves today, but comparatively speaking, the patient today has a voice in their diagnosis, care, and overall treatment approach that was completely foreign to the patient of that era. Susan had also been accustomed to taking every word her psychologists said for decades as the Gospel, so advisement of medical professionals was similarly inerrant according to her worldview.

For those in Susan's generation, especially women, what medical professionals said went. Recommendations today are just that—recommendations or suggestions that patients often are given the opportunity to informatively consider. Recommendations then were more like commands with little to no explicit informed consent, whether or not intended as such. It was the old "just trust us, we're the professionals" routine. And Susan did.

The treatment options for pituitary dwarfism in the 1960s and 1970s were neither plentiful nor commonplace. Tim was evaluated by a series of specialists and initially they prescribed steroids and testosterone supplementation to support his growth. Their efficacy was limited. Susan was weary from chasing answers only to find more questions about Tim's trajectory. Finally, in 1970, an answer seemed to fall in Susan's lap.

A Miracle Drug

Hormone therapy was emerging within the medical community as a viable option for certain conditions, and scientists had an innovative hormonal theory to test. All they needed was a little help from dead people. "A hormone collected from the brains of dead persons is making dwarfed children grow, a physician reported Friday," *The San Bernardino County Sun* reported in 1958. It sounds like another one of Roger Corman's sci-fi cult classics starring Susan Cabot, but even though Susan ultimately had a leading role in the ordeal, it was all real life.

Human growth hormone (HGH) has been of interest to the medical field since the early 1910s, but in the 1940s, concentrated study began on isolating HGH. The study was significant in treatment options for those who were HGH-deficient with diagnoses such as certain types of dwarfism and other endocrine diseases. Scientific breakthrough for HGH came in 1956 when Dr. Li and Dr. Papkoff of the University of California and Dr. Raben of The New England Medical Center in Boston successfully isolated the growth hormone from the human pituitary gland. Before 1956, monkeys were used in experiments conducted on hormonal enzymes involved in growth and how those processes might be replicated organically or synthetically to assist children deficient in HGH to grow on a more uninhibited growth curve.

Dr. Raben was one of the first medical experts to use HGH isolation successfully in the treatment of HGH-deficient children. After purifying the enzymes taken from cadavers no longer in need of their own HGH, a serum was produced with said enzymes and administered through injection therapy. One of Dr. Raben's first patients to receive the HGH injections was a thirteen-year-old girl whose growth had stunted after a tumor ravaged her own pituitary gland's organic growth process.

Though it's not usually something we like to think about, the use of cadavers in medical education and research dates back to ancient times. Cadavers have long since provided an invaluable resource for anatomical study, surgical training, and the advancement of medical knowledge in general. Despite the ethical concerns surrounding their use, cadavers have played a crucial role in shaping modern medicine both for good and for bad. It was an arduous process to extract HGH from dead bodies, but it was a superior means compared to the previously used monkey pituitary glands.

Dr. Raben's thirteen-year-old patient grew more than an inch in six weeks post-treatment. This child was one of the thousands from 1958 until 1985 to be experimentally treated with this breakthrough discovery serum through the National Hormone and Pituitary Program. For nearly three decades, a series of studies were conducted with patients of all ages from around the globe who suffered from insufficient pituitary gland function. And for years, the results were promising and backed by the greatest minds in science and medicine.

Under the advisement of Tim's specialists, Susan consented to Tim's participation in an experimental HGH study intended to boost his body's own hormone-producing process. The study itself didn't sound particularly different from the prescribed medication Tim was already taking; with the limited outcomes of his regimen at the time the study was suggested to Susan, and signing him up for these experimental injections seemed to be the next right step.

At age six, Tim received his first HGH injection. It was an unmentionable amount of serum injected into his body that was as casually given as a multivitamin or aspirin would have been. These injections had been deemed safe enough to administer to children, and they gave parents an enormous amount of hope. "Most parents had to stand on their heads to get treatment…this was a way for him to be like everyone else…we saw this as a chance to make something that could be a handicap not have to be a handicap," Mrs. Coussan, whose son was also a participant in the same study as Tim, told the *Los Angeles Times*.

Reportedly, thousands of dead brains had to be used in order to extract just a few drops of HGH, which was the primary ingredient of the serum injected into study participants. Things went along swimmingly for quite some time after the global studies initially returned few side effects and substantial successes. Children grew taller, began gaining healthy weight and muscle mass, and in many instances, self-confidence.

The studies certainly meant tremendous advancement for the field of endocrinology, but many scientists began theorizing about HGH's benefits for other areas of medicine. HGH's receptors are responsible for dozens of biological processes, and these studies showed improvement in glucose metabolism, cardiac function, and even showed promise in the treatment of certain types of cancers. For thousands, it was a miracle drug for which they were praising the heavens.

By the early 1980s, this miracle drug had collided with an ethical dilemma. Because of the countless worldwide successes being reported about HGH, many parents went to their physicians with requests for HGH's cosmetic benefits. Many thought that adding a few inches to their child's height might boost their self-confidence and general acceptance in life. The parents who initially enrolled in the experimental studies on HGH allowed their children to participate based on a mutually agreed-upon necessity with their child's physicians and not for reasons of "cosmetic endocrinology." The cosmetic benefits of "growing taller" later emerged from the promising results as a commodity of its own, resulting in a trend of unsolicited inquiries from parents of shorter children.

The Missoulian's Paul Raeburn reported in October 1984:

Human growth hormone to compensate for natural deficiencies has been so rare it was reserved for youngsters whose own bodies lacked it. Now, through genetic engineering, the substance soon may be available in unlimited quantities. Doctors expect enormous demand from otherwise healthy people who want to be taller and stronger. But thereby hangs a serious dilemma. Should it be freely prescribed for all comers?

The natural production of HGH tends to naturally decrease in the body with age, so the promise of rejuvenation through HGH injections became a fad in both sports and cosmetic fields. Athletes often used HGH injections to secure an edge over competitors in strength, vitality, and muscle mass. There were also reports of cosmetic experts who espoused the usage of HGH injections for their anti-aging capabilities. In more recent years, the usage of HGH has been placed under strict governmental guidelines because of its potency and potential to wreak havoc on physiological processes within the human body if misused.

Lawsuits: Parents v. Science

By 1985, the insidious underbelly of the miracle drug that took the world by storm began to show, and it involved much more than an ethical dilemma of cosmetics. Three healthy young men suddenly died of the extremely rare brain-eating condition Creutzfeldt-Jakob Disease (CJD). The first victim of CJD was a twenty-year-old who died in November of 1984. The second victim was a twenty-two-year-old who died in April of 1985. The third was a thirty-four-year-old who died in February of 1985. These three cases were perplexing to medical professionals who feared an epidemic of some kind with the deadly prion often synonymous with "mad-cow disease." CJD was discovered in the 1920s, but has always been considered a very rare condition, infecting one or two people per million each year.

All medical eyes were on the case of the three American men who suddenly contracted CJD and died within a few weeks of their diagnoses. Upon further investigation of their profiles, a singular shared experience in the files of all three was unignorable. As young children, the three had each participated in the experimental HGH studies.

Upon finding the connection to the study, experiments were immediately discontinued as scientists scrambled to determine exactly *how* CJD was connected to the serum and how extensive the damage was. In the wake of the fiasco, biotech giant Genentech filled in the gap for those still in need of HGH. The company began formulating a synthetic form of HGH that would no longer require the assistance of dead brain tissue. It was cheaper, easier to make, and didn't come with as many inherent risks.

Though CJD was the deadliest of the injections' side effects, it was just one of many issues eventually found. Many of the diseases cadavers had in life remained in their tissues in death. So whatever diseased elements the cadavers had were infused into the healthy tissues of the living study participants. Unfortunately, the side effects often lay dormant for years before being detected, and once detected, there was little recourse available, turning patients into victims in a single diagnosis.

The investigation into the series of studies conducted on HGH found the CJD prion was derived from one or more cadavers infected with the disease, unbeknownst to those responsible for the extraction process. After enzymes were retrieved, they reportedly went through a series of purification processes in university laboratories across the globe, but CJD was resistant to all purification efforts.

The investigation also assessed how widespread the contamination was. In tracing the profiles of the three young American men who died, they were able to determine the time frame, laboratory, and distribution batch with which they were associated. The damage was widespread, as more than 25,000 people worldwide had the potential for exposure. The exact number of deaths related to the contamination is unknown, but many speculate CJD claimed the lives of more than 5,000 people who participated in the HGH studies.

Tim was among the percentage of those eventually found to be infected with CJD, nearly two decades after he received the injections at age six. It is unknown whether all parents (Susan included) were initially informed that the hormones extracted to create the serum were cadaver derivatives. Though for some desperate enough, it wouldn't have made a difference where the serum came from as long as their child was accepted into the study for this "miracle" treatment. Reportedly, many parents were given a scant summary of the study's particulars that conveniently left out the whole "this stuff is coming from dead bodies" point, though it is unknown how detailed the summary given specifically to Susan was. Years later, of course, everyone knew the derivative nature of the serum and the horrific implications of that, but in the 1970s, informed consent was altogether different than it is today. So, when Susan signed on the dotted line for Tim's participation, it's anyone's guess as to how clearly she understood what *exactly* she was agreeing to, and certainly *no one* was aware of the presence of contamination until years later. To her, and many like her, she was signing her child up for the most promising treatment option in modern science—and the safest.

Though the general thrust of the study just described may seem preposterous and science-fictionish to us now, at the time, what was proposed to Susan and thousands of others was considered a serious scientific study backed by serious scientific minds to weigh the benefits and risks of such a game-changing potential treatment. Just as the medieval bloodletting seems like a common-sense no-no to us today, at the time, "experts" were using all the information they had available to them and "practicing medicine" in determining what worked and what didn't work for myriad human conditions. The same was true for the study in which Tim was a part.

With regard to Susan and Tim, the ominous whisperings of the experimental HGH study only came into play when Tim's usage of the injections was implicated in Susan's brutal murder. Of course, the parallel between the experimental injections featured in *Wasp Woman* and those she administered to Tim within the context of the HGH study also didn't do anything but fuel imaginations.

During the press hurricanes surrounding Tim's trials, mentions of *Wasp Woman* did nothing but incite images of dark experimental labs with potions and needles hidden behind a trick bookcase, but the truth was, the study was legitimate at the time, based on the most up-to-date information available to scientists, physicians, and patients. Susan and Tim were far from the only ones who suffered from the downfalls of that particular series of experimental studies, though given Susan's career, their story was probably the most publicized. True, it was one of science's best examples of an experiment gone wrong for thousands, but the "creepy" element was grossly exaggerated due to the media's connection with Susan's on-screen portrayal of "Janice Starlin" as the youth-obsessed CEO who dabbles in a mad-scientist lab with mysterious injections of a green hue.

Susan loved Tim fiercely, and did nearly everything possible to give him a chance at a "normal" life, but according to her second husband, Michael Roman, she also harbored immense shame over Tim's condition:

> *Here you had an extremely creative individual [Susan], and the greatest thing that a woman can create is another life, that literally comes out of her. And this artistic person creates this life…and the life is flawed. Can you imagine? The anger, the desperation, the fear, the anxiety, the mixed feelings? "The greatest thing I could create is a life, and this life is flawed! There's something wrong with it!" So, what she was trying to do was just*

protect this precious creation that she created, came out of her, and that's where she was so protective of him.

During Tim's first trial for the death of his mother, Deputy District Attorney Bradford E. Stone said, "I think Roman is just a statistic that went bad."

Chapter Five
A Family at Last

"Families are messy. Immortal families are eternally messy. Sometimes the best we can do is to remind each other that we're related for better or for worse...and try to keep the maiming and killing to a minimum."

— Rick Riordan, *The Sea of Monsters*

Though her primary focus was on motherhood, in the late 1960s and early 1970s, Susan was still accepting the occasional television role in shows like *Bracken's World, Owen Marshall, Counselor at Law,* and the daytime soap opera *The Brighter Day*, as well as some commercial work. While Tim was either at school during the day or being cared for by carefully vetted nannies in the evenings, Susan also taught acting classes.

During Tim's first few years, Susan protected herself and him by avoiding the dating scene she once was so involved in. She gave the old "I'm trying to work things out with my British diplomat ex-husband and it's messy" routine. It was a harmless enough story to keep those of the male persuasion at arm's length, and to presumably "explain" Tim. But there was one tall, dark, handsome guy who didn't care as much about "messy" as other potential suitors.

In 1968, Susan was filling in for another teacher in an evening class when an attractive young student filed in with his peers and found himself captivated by his substitute teacher, "Ms. Cabot." Hollywood hopeful Michael Roman was twenty-five years old and became more and more enchanted by his older, single teacher as the first night of class went on. Susan was forty, still beautiful and well-kempt, and despite her somewhat choppy, linear career, was known as an industry professional for her contract days and acting resume, which to acting hopefuls like Michael was very impressive. She knew her stuff both on stage and on screen and was considered an acting expert, however brief her time in the limelight had been.

Michael was born in Hungary but had lived in the States for years before meeting Susan. He had just completed his Army National Guard service when he enrolled in college, and as an elective chose acting in consideration of a career in the field. Michael told Tom Weaver in an interview he was terribly nervous that first class under Susan, and when she worked with him individually. Even before the end of the first week of class, Michael said he knew he wanted to marry her. She was not only an expert when it came to the mechanics and art of acting, she was kind and earnest in her instruction of Michael.

Michael asked Susan to marry him ten days after that first private acting lesson, and according to Susan, it was a "spiritual union." Susan was a mystic at heart and had a deep veneration for all world regions. Through her lifelong spiritual wrestling, she identified most closely with her ethnoreligious roots of Judaism, but she enjoyed discussing and writing about various theologies. Eventually, she landed somewhere between Judaism and Christianity in her own practice. Both being seasoned conversationalists, Michael and Susan spent much of their first dates discussing their faiths and philosophies.

Michael and Susan eloped to Las Vegas and married. Though Michael was young and had no children of his own, he seemed to understand the complexities of Susan's situation with Tim and her mother, Muriel, who was by that point living with Susan and Tim. Michael acquired an instant family when he and Susan married, and even in his mid-twenties, he offered nearly as much compassion to Tim and Muriel's quirks as Susan did. Michael told Tom Weaver that Muriel was a "good-hearted, loving person," and just wild about Tim, but she drove Susan crazy with her constant chatter and reminiscences about the past.

Susan was reportedly good to her mother despite their years apart, but Michael said having both Tim *and* Muriel under the same roof was like Susan having two children to raise.

Michael claimed Susan never offered any information surrounding the issue of Tim's biological father. Whoever the guy was, it was obvious he wasn't around, but Susan offered no explanation. Michael began to care deeply for Tim, who was five years old when he married Susan. Just after the two married, Michael officially adopted Tim and he became "Timothy Cabot Roman." The Romans plus Muriel would make a patchwork family in Susan's Encino mansion for the next decade.

Timothy Scott Roman

For much of his formative years, Tim was coddled by Susan and Muriel both, while Michael was the more liberal voice in wanting to push him toward more independence and "normalcy." The subject of "Tim" and how he should be raised was a contentious one among all three adults in the home. Everyone had their own ideas on how Tim's elementary and middle school years should be approached, on everything from sleepovers and girlfriends to Boy Scouts and cotillion classes.

When Tim was six years old, Susan and Michael (as Tim's newly instated father) moved forward with signing for his participation in the growth hormone study, hoping he would benefit from the experiment in catching up with his peers in more conventional development. It was slow at first, but eventually, there were changes in Tim. He certainly didn't sprout inches overnight, but in the following weeks and months, he began filling out, picking up weight, and growing sturdier. Initially, Susan took Tim for the injections in-clinic with routine follow-ups to evaluate his system's response to the newly introduced drug. He seemed to have no immediate negative side effects except maybe some initial fatigue and upset stomach. After the first several injections were administered with no obvious ill effects, Tim's medical team and his parents were pleased with the changes—however small at first—they were seeing. It wasn't magic, but it seemed like the best option for a once hopeless situation.

After Susan's death, many claimed that she herself began taking the injections, though Michael Roman and Tom Weaver both vehemently deny that. Again, drawing from the parallels in *Wasp Woman*, even close girlfriends of Susan's swore she must have taken the injections to appear younger, just like "Janice Starlin" had in Corman's film. But the hypodermics rationed to her through prescription held no youth serum. They held a carefully formulated *growth* serum. It is highly doubtful that Susan Cabot Roman, at age forty-three, wanted to *grow* any. Susan was neither delusional about the effects of the experimental drug that she had been medically advised to sign for, nor would she have played fast and loose with Tim's care.

Further, this was an experimental study with rigid parameters. Undoubtedly, Tim's specialists would have noticed a little thing like his mother perpetually "running out of serum and requesting more" if she, in fact, were dosing herself or overdosing him. If that had been true, Tim would have been most likely removed from the study, and Tim's physicians would have reported Susan to the child welfare authorities for a whole host of issues.

Susan's autopsy showed no evidence of any drugs, such as those in the serum. The only medication in her system at the time of her death was the bronchodilator Theophylline she was prescribed for asthmatic symptoms. We know from Tim's experience (along with the thousands of other patients who were exposed to the contamination in that particular batch) that any fluid or tissue contact with the drug would have eventually developed CJD, too. If Susan did take the injections at any point or was even accidentally exposed by a prick, she too would have contracted CJD. Her autopsy showed no evidence of degenerative diseases of any nature.

Susan's friends and family did notice a change in her demeanor in the 1970s around the same time Tim began receiving the injections. She *was* having a reaction to hormonal stimuli much like Tim, but it was no diabolical mystery. What actually happened was a little thing called menopause.

On the Rocks

The 1970s brought a significant shift in Hollywood's culture and productions. This decade saw the rise of a new generation of filmmakers who challenged traditional storytelling conventions and pushed the boundaries of what was considered acceptable on screen. Directors like Martin Scorsese, Francis Ford Coppola, and Steven Spielberg emerged as leading figures, bringing a fresh perspective and an auteur sensibility to their films. The 1970s also witnessed the rise of the blockbuster, with films like *Jaws* and *Star Wars* that revolutionized the way movies were made and marketed. Additionally, this era saw the emergence of new genres, such as the gritty crime drama and the socially conscious film. These changes left many former Hollywood contract players in Susan's generation feeling like dinosaurs with no remaining viable connection to the industry.

Susan worked outside her Encino home very little in the 1970s, but she continued to paint in her home studio. She did, however, appear in an episode of Dorothy Kingsley's television show *Bracken's World* (One, Two, Three…Cry) as a support character. She still had regular luncheons with girlfriends and maintained her usual phone chats with legions of friends as she always had, but menopause coinciding with less work for an aging starlet turned to depressive insecurity. Susan was born beautiful and had often relied on her stunning bone structure, finite facial features, and slim physique in her career and sociality. Her hormonal changes were brutal to her self-esteem, and she became increasingly insecure in her appearance. What Hollywood starlet doesn't experience the career crisis of aging at some point? She began obsessing over her skin care and exaggerating her eyeliner in compensation—something that drove Michael up a wall. He told Tom Weaver:

...she would overdo her makeup. And the reason she did that is, she was afraid, she was bashful, and this was a security blanket, she put all these layers or—my word—masks, that she was hiding behind! She didn't need 'em. Did not need 'em at all. It broke my heart to see that happen.

She experienced degrees of what many who go through the dreaded "M" word experience: mood swings, hot flashes, insomnia, insecurity, emotionality, weight gain, fatigue, etc. And it often made for uncomfortable dynamics in the home because the usually vibrant, caretaking Susan was suddenly distant and irritable.

When Susan and Michael married, she had a hormonal intrauterine device (IUD) implanted to avoid future pregnancies. IUDs were in their infancy in the United States in the 1960s and 1970s, and their potential side effects weren't as well-understood as they are today (i.e. the nightmare of the Dalkon Shield). Susan certainly battled depression and anxiety for decades under the care of both physicians and psychologists, but given the timeline of the hormonal dance with the implantation of the more "primitive" Saf T Coil IUD, plus the onset of menopause at forty-three, it isn't exactly far-fetched for her to have had a marked uptick in depression and anxiety symptoms.

Michael and Susan's marriage took a savage turn in the mid-seventies, with competing flames of intensity in their mutual love and accumulating resentment of each other. In Susan's insecurity, she began to feel threatened by the fifteen-year age difference between herself and Michael. Michael was consummately devoted and innocently saw her as the same beautiful woman he always had, but it was difficult for her to hear his reassurance with her plummeting self-esteem and the few extra pounds she had acquired. The Romans were constantly in and out of marriage therapy with Susan's longtime psychologist, Dr. Carl Faber.

Carl Faber, PhD

The turmoil of the 1960s brought immense sociopolitical change, in part through activism for civil rights and anti-war campaigns in the midst of the

Vietnam War. The decade witnessed the emergence of the hippie counterculture that rejected mainstream values and embraced peace, love, and freedom as guiding principles. This movement had a profound effect on American society in the correlative erosion of systematic hierarchy. Throughout the 1960s and 1970s, the beaded "feel good" rhetoric had an increasingly concentrated presence in the field of entertainment and "pop psychology."

In breaking down the more traditional approach to mental health, Dr. Carl Faber's "groovy vibes" appealed to many like Susan, who had long felt the oppression of systematic conventionality in medicine and mental health. Faber's balmy, easy-going personality was the antithesis of the stereotypical "Freudian" psychoanalyst with rigid approaches toward the doctor-patient relationship. Faber (who preferred his clients call him "Carl") was more of a "friend" to his clients with his flexible, non-traditional scope and inextinguishable degree of understanding. Faber literally and metaphorically replaced the winged-back armchair of psychologists who had preceded him with a rocking chair from which he conducted his therapy sessions. From the 1960s until his death in 1996, Dr. Carl Faber was a god in the eyes of many.

A California native, Faber was a trendy "pop psychologist" in Westwood, California, for over three decades. He often lectured at the University of California, Los Angeles (UCLA) on a variety of social and interpersonal issues from divorce, parenting, and drug addiction to codependency, depression, and emotional injury. Faber had curious patchwork ideologies drawn from new-age spirituality, sexuality, and Jungian principles, and seemed more interested in fluid esoteric discussions than empiricism.

The 1960s brought America's second wave of feminism, and Faber gallantly developed several lecture series about "helping women escape slavery." His so-called feministic work drew sharp criticism from feminists who claimed he was pandering to women from his seat of White male privilege. Many feminists condemned his lectures on "women in slavery" as chauvinistic propaganda, though he vehemently denied espousing such values.

Carl Faber thought of himself as a social justice activist with progressive ideals on humanity's intricate struggles. In his practice, he had a special interest in relational dynamics in what he called "sex wars," and claimed to be an avid "female sympathizer." "I would say I am more sympathetic with women than men," Faber said.

Faber claimed his mother struggled with lifelong depression and used him as her constant sounding board when he was a child. He said his father maintained very chauvinistic ideals, but he himself had evolved from those and "understood the plight of women."

"I know what it's like for you," he would say to his female lecture audiences and clients. "I was responsible to take care of my mother since I was born," he said. He believed because of the codependent relationship he had with his mother when he was a child, he had some kind of psychic insight into the feminine experience.

During a recorded lecture in the 1970s, one female feminist in attendance openly rebuked Faber for his "sexist attitude" in claiming he was "*the man who knew why women are oppressed and which roads to follow in order to not be oppressed….. [but] it's the woman's road.*"

Despite his work's criticism, he maintained a loyal fanbase made up of mostly women who considered him a brilliant intuitive, who knew exactly what women felt and needed. Susan was a longtime client of Faber's and a committed member of his fanbase. Susan hung on every word "Carl" said and wrote. She fervently believed in his healing power and religiously practiced his teachings. Susan's favorite work of Faber's was his 1976 book called *On Listening*:

> *Most people have never really been listened to. They live in a lonely silence---no one knowing what they feel, how they live, or what they have done. They are prisoners of the eyes of others, of the stereotyped, limited, superficial and often distorted ways that others see them. There are no words to adequately describe what it is to be free with another person. It is most often a sensing that someone will let us be all of what we are at that moment. We can talk about whatever we wish, express in any way whatever feelings are in our hearts. We can take as much*

time as we need. We can sit, stand, pace, yell, cry, pound the floor, dance, or weep for joy. Whatever and however we are at the moment is accepted and respected. When someone really listens to us, our blood flows in his or her veins. That person is moved as we are by our history, passions, hurts, binds, values, joys; in short, by the integrity of our existence. It is an uncritical experience. We are blood sisters, blood brothers, friends of the blood. The blood carries an understanding beyond ideas. The listener's instinct to observe and judge is transcended.

Faber never really cared much for engaging in empirical studies or discussing his topics from a scholarly perspective. Instead, he published books of rambling, feel-good poetry and seemed to use his own life experiences rather than his academic training to "help" others overcome their difficulties. He spoke at churches, coffee shops, and universities, and he built a brand as a benevolent icon. A description of his lecture series on "emotional slavery" from UCLA's catalogue is described as:

The first in a series with Dr. Carl A. Faber exploring the experience and healing of emotional slavery. Encouraged by selfishness, ignorance, and 'ageism,' countless children are brought into the world serving as slaves for others. As slaves, they are neither experienced nor treated with dignity as separate persons. In this essential rape of personal dignity, slaves come to feel the needs and hurts of others more than they feel their own. As slaves gain competence at being slaves, more persons are attracted to exploit their vulnerabilities and exaggerated empathy. The logical development of this is a lifetime of wearying, suicidal struggle to please and placate several slave owners viciously competing for the slave's services and 'love.' Because of the depth of injury to dignity and the consequent lack of any natural sense of privacy and personal rights, emancipation from slavery is very difficult. Knowledge and consciousness alone are seldom sufficient to liberate emotional slaves. Freedom usually requires longer years of learning, therapy, and good relationships than do other psychological problems. Often a self-chosen 'kidnapping' by loving friends and therapists is required to restore injured dignity. Only then can the inevitable outrageous revenges and 'cold treatments' of slave owners be handled without overwhelming guilt and self-doubt.

Faber was calm and kind with soft monotones of acceptance. There was some kind of addictive quality to Faber's private sessions, as many of his clients (both male and female) attended weekly sessions with him for decades. He was hailed as a towering professional in the field of psychology more by his clients than his colleagues. He was mostly cliches and drugstore psychology mixed with new age principles, and he often used his platform to talk about his own personal issues and opinions. Faber described himself as "a loner who helped other loners" in his practice, and often became close personal friends with his clients outside of therapy sessions.

Having known Susan for more than twenty years, Faber was called as a key witness in Tim's trials for his intimate knowledge of Susan, Michael, Tim, and the dynamics of their relationships. Somehow, all his lofty feministic philosophies slipped his mind on the witness stand, as he helped paint Susan's portrait as a maniacal mother who, like Faber's own mother, had subjected Tim to a lifetime of "emotional slavery" akin to that which Faber so often lectured on.

Faber's narrow view of the Romans' relational dynamics was centered on the misogynist belief that if Susan had just "gotten it together," the family wouldn't have been suffering with constant turmoil. Dr. Paula J. Caplan is a pioneer in the scholarly study of mother-blaming within society. As a longtime clinician, Caplan said her reason for initially researching the phenomenon of mother-blaming was during her early clinical work with families when she noticed a disturbing trend: "I noticed that no matter what was wrong, no matter what the reason for the family's coming to the clinic, it turned out the mother was always assumed to be responsible for the problem."

✠✠✠

As Tim grew, so did his physical and behavioral challenges. Whether related to the injections, his prematurity, or plain old immovable genetics, Tim suffered with epilepsy throughout his childhood. He also exhibited odd, unpredictable behaviors including aggressive outbursts that suggested neurological disconnects doctors couldn't provide ready answers for. While the injections did in fact boost his growth, he was still much shorter than his peers. He did not proportionately look like a person with dwarfism, but he was very small and never outgrew his "baby face." He was cute with dark brown hair and eyes like his mother, and well-kempt with the latest fashions and hairstyles. Being a part of an experimental study that used cadaver enzymes conjures a host of sideshow images, but Tim appeared "normal" except for his short stature.

His behavior, however, was a separate issue. Tom Weaver once described Tim as Susan's "aggressively oddball son." He said, "The kid was pleasant, but… strange. He struck me as looking about twelve years old (facially and height-wise), but he was obviously much older, because he had his own car." While Tim tried to be socially connected in middle and high school, he faced pervasive bullying from the boys and rejection from the girls. Cognitively, there were reportedly delays, and he often struggled through his schoolwork requirements causing him to drop behind a year.

Tim was high maintenance all the way around, and the demands of his care at home seemed to increase as he aged. Puberty was especially challenging for him, given the already delicate balance of his hormones. Though he was medically stable with his most obvious symptoms managed by medication in high school, emotionally, he required a lot from Susan. Tim was moody and prone to violent outbursts. His unpredictability was draining for them both. One minute, he would curl up on Susan in a crying heap over the latest bullying incident at school, and the next, he would lash out at her or the dogs for some perceived slight. By high school, Tim had reached 5'5, but he had enough anger in him to convince anyone he was every inch of 7'7 when he was triggered. There was undoubtedly a part of Susan that was afraid of Tim.

Susan tried to help Tim channel his aggression through regular therapy sessions and martial arts classes after he showed such an interest in Bruce Lee films. He became proficient in the art and developed a deep ardor for

Asian culture. He also engaged in weightlifting, for which Susan purchased elaborate home gym equipment for him.

Whether intentional or not, Susan enabled his reliance on her, because one, she loved him, and two, she depended on his dependence. It was difficult for her to break the patterns established early in her motherhood that set her up as Tim's only and constant caregiver. Due to his medical fragility in his first few years of life, her helicoptering is essentially what helped him survive.

Though she was eventually able to lead him toward independence when he started school, that leading stalled by the time he reached high school, when Susan's own mental health declined with the onset of menopause. With his volatility as a teenager and her own depressed state, it was easier to revert to his early years when she was his constant aid.

According to nearly all sources, Tim was spoiled and had little concept of reality, as Susan ran interference for him in matters of inconvenience and/or difficulty. Susan loved him, and like all parents, wanted the best for him, but as he grew older, he began escalating to a level of sovereignty in their Encino home. What Tim wanted, he got, no matter how unreasonable.

Whether more related to his complex medical history or the way he had been parented, his behavior reached unmanageable levels for the whole household. Muriel had moved out to an apartment of her own by 1980, and Michael and Susan were in weekly marriage therapy. The house was tense with emotional reactivity, and all three Romans were walking a tightrope. All three were in individual and joint counseling sessions with psychiatrists and psychologists, but Dr. Faber's advice only kept the three coming back for more and more sessions. Susan had grown very dependent on his interpretation of her life and life in general after years of seeing him regularly. Dr. Faber and Tim seemed to have more control in Michael and Susan's marriage than either one of them did.

One of the only bright spots of the early 1970s for Susan was when she took the stage again for a role of light opera. In the Summer of 1973, she appeared in the off-Broadway musical *Camelot* starring John Raitt as "King

Arthur." Susan was Raitt's leading lady as the King's "sprightly and beautiful" "Queen Guenevere." The show ran for seven nights at Broadway at Music Circus in Sacramento. Susan reveled in the reconnection with her first love of music and hated to see the end of the run. Susan thrived when she was steadily working, but in an unpredictable industry fraught with ageism, steady work was harder to come by.

The need for relational intervention mounted for all three Romans as Tim aged. The sole focus of the Roman family became Tim, and Susan and Michael soon felt like strangers to each other—angry strangers. Susan believed she alone knew what was best for Tim, while Michael naively provided the more objective perspective of Tim's boyhood experience.

Susan could give two million and one reasons why it could be potentially dangerous for Tim to join the Boy Scouts, while Michael insisted a boy should "toughen up" through normal boyhood experiences. One argument about Boy Scouts isn't so bad, but when the tensions accumulate from constant, minute-to-minute arguments of a similar nature, relational catastrophe is inevitable, especially without solid resourcing.

Unfortunately, the Romans' primary source of "help" was "Carl," who "understood," but offered nothing in the way of practicalities like building up each of the Romans' coping skills, communication strategies, and interpersonal boundaries. Faber's main therapeutic thrust was the exploration of childhood emotional injuries, but he also liked to mix other modalities into his therapeutic caldron, like Freud's dream analysis and Jung's theory on repressed memories. These elements are great, but perhaps not as useful to people in dire straits as the Romans were. All three were in critical emotional states and perpetually on the verge of volcanic eruptions while Faber merely coached them twice a week in his "feministic" opinions on marriage, parenting, and "slavery." He often turned sessions into extensions of his lectures on principles such as those detailed in his lecture series called "Woman as Slave," described on the original transcript as follows:

> *This is the third episode 'Sexuality, violence, and aggression' in a four part series of lectures by Dr. Carl Faber entitled "Woman as slave." This*

episode is in two parts. Part one is Faber's lecture on sexuality, violence, and aggression, given in January 1977. Dr. Carl Faber, a heterosexual monogamist, lectures on how, with awareness, women may get sexually spaced out, allowing sex with no closeness some feel is 'mature.' They may be turned off completely and may become sexually involved with a person they trust: a woman. Faber goes on to suggest that when a woman gets in touch with how men have treated her, she experiences a violent murderous homicidal rage without end. In the end, she can learn physical self-protection and respect.

These perspectives and similar ones of Faber's don't seem particularly helpful for families in real-time relationship crises, but the three Romans continued to schedule sessions with him religiously for the entire span of Susan and Michael's marriage.

Susan had great difficulty admitting she had essentially done all she could do for Tim by the time he graduated high school at nineteen. He was high-functioning in basic self-care and daily chores around the house and had mastered many aspects of his martial arts classes, driving, gardening, sketching and painting like his mother, and dog training, but emotionally, he was like a living, breathing time bomb.

Chapter Six
Drying Inward from the Edge

"I know what my heart is like since your love died: It is like a hollow ledge holding a little pool left there by the tide, a little tepid pool, drying inward from the edge."

— *Ebb* by Edna St. Vincent Millay

"I love you, but I, I, I, I, I, I can't *live* with you!" Michael finally admitted to Susan, sitting across from him in therapy. Forty pounds had just been lifted off of his chest. He said the thing to her and no bolt of lightning, no gut punch, nothing. He survived the admission. She sat cold and flat as his words sank in. It was painful to hear of course, but certainly not shocking to Susan. They both knew something had to give. Susan filed for divorce in December of 1980 after twelve years of marriage. She was fifty-three and Michael was thirty-eight. Susan found herself a single mother again—this time not to an infant, but to a sixteen-year-old boy.

Michael moved out as Susan coolly resided detached in another part of the house. It was incredibly emotional for Michael to leave the family he had loved and grown with for the last twelve years, however necessary he deemed their decision to part ways at the time. Because of the cloud of depression that had fallen on Susan, she had already emotionally resigned to their split and everything it would mean. Michael had been one of the only stable forces in her whole lifetime and she truly loved him, but there was too much friction, resentment, and too much Dr. Faber and Tim for them to vulnerably repair what needed repairing.

The only thing Susan asked Michael for in the divorce was $225.00 monthly child support and for Michael to retain her and Tim on his medical insurance. Michael obliged and remained involved in Tim's life despite the rupture. Occasionally, he and Susan communicated, but mostly about Tim's care and activities. By the Fall of 1981, the season of the Romans was over.

With Michael gone, Susan's energy became hyper-focused on teenage Tim. Susan wasn't working in the 1980s partly because of her depression and anxiety, partly because of Tim's constant needs, and partly because Hollywood rarely goes out of its way to open doors for aging starlets. She kept in touch with her social circle and continued painting in her in-home studio, but there was a sense of lethargy about her that had largely replaced her former vibrance. After the divorce, she merely went through the motions of life.

It isn't psychotic, of course, to experience an increase in the blues after a significant life change such as a divorce, but in the media's narrow perspective of hype, somewhere along the line Susan's "blues" turned into a series of mental breakdowns in "Norma Desmond" fashion. And media audiences are much more intrigued by "Norma Desmond" stuff than circumstantial blues, aren't we?

Tim continued to struggle with school both academically and socially as he neared graduation. It never seemed to get any easier for him despite his and Susan's best efforts. There were days when Tim was terrified to go to school because of the harassment that sometimes escalated to his physical harm. His competence in martial arts was really only theoretically helpful to him. In his room late at night, he rehearsed what he really wanted to say or do when bullies confronted him, but in the heat of the moment on campus, he was all thumbs and stutters. As a loner, Tim used his lunch time to hang out in the library outside the always "accidental" shoves and taunting.

Sometimes his bullies would wait for him to leave the library on his way to his next class and use those few yards to terrorize him. Tim had told Susan of his dreaded "after-lunch walk" and in desperation, she would sometimes go to school and walk with Tim from the library to his next class to ward off any awaiting bullies. Having his famous mother who was obviously very conspicuous walk him around campus only gave his peers more reason to target him, but at least the walk from the library kept additional physical confrontations at bay.

Not only was Susan protective of Tim and cried nearly as much as he did when she would ice his shiners or wipe his bloody nose after school, but she herself knew the shame of bullying and being discriminated against in the studio system because of her height. She and Michael both had talked ad nauseam with Tim's teachers and principal, but their "zero tolerance bullying policy" only went so far. Susan even considered pulling Tim out on several occasions and hiring a private tutor to ensure he could graduate, but she knew that would only be a band-aid and Tim would suffer in other ways if he were kept completely from the outside world. It was easier for Susan to physically discourage Tim's bullies on his walks to class than to trust the school to prevent further attacks.

In 1984, Tim began attending public community college Los Angeles Pierce College in Woodland Hills after high school. He majored in biochemistry but chose art courses for his electives. One testimony given during Tim's trial indicated Susan encouraged Tim's interest in chemistry as a future career option. His college instructor, Dr. John Watkins, told her it was unrealistic for her to believe Tim would be scholastically capable of doing anything with chemistry beyond passing grades in community college. Susan argued with Dr. Watkins all the way, assuring him that Tim could, in fact, become an esteemed chemist if he set his mind to it. "[Susan] thought that [Tim] could be very advanced and kind of a scholar in biology and subjects like that. When, in fact, he was really struggling to graduate from high school," Dr. Watkins stated from the witness stand during Tim's second trial. Tim's (second) attorney, Michael White, asked Dr. Watkins: "Now, did you have a conversation with the mother concerning this report?" Dr. Watkins answered: "Yes, I did. In a very detailed conversation with her, I also referred him for tutoring and he received tutoring after that."

Though the defense tried to use this example of Tim's aptitude as evidence of Susan's delusional state, her argument with Dr. Watkins, however, was more of an advocacy effort for Tim. After that meeting, she arranged for a tutor named Michael Carter to come to their home and help Tim boost his grades beyond merely passing. Obviously, if Susan had truly been delusional about what Tim was capable of, she would never have hired a private tutor to help him excel. She knew Tim was different and struggled with many dimensions of life, but her philosophy on Tim was always: "After all, some small people have done some mighty big things, men and women alike."

Tim didn't have loads of friends, but in college, he had more than he had in high school and the years of bullying he had suffered under suddenly lifted. He would infrequently have friends over to their house, and Susan would be the over-perfumed, charming hostess as she had been in her glory days. Tim's friends reportedly found her to be captivating and kind, but oddly over-the-top with her mothering that seemed disproportionate for a man in his twenties. Tim also dated infrequently. Despite many reports, Susan was not threatened by Tim dating in the traditional sense of a mother being threatened by her son's coming-of-age interest in the opposite sex. She was concerned about Tim's general impulsivity and underdeveloped sense of interpersonal engagement. She also did not want him to get hurt if his date declined an advance or subsequent date in a less-than-sensitive way. Before Susan's death, Tim's dating life only consisted of a handful of "first" dates with girls just as socially awkward as he was.

The experimental injections were a thing of the almost forgotten past, though according to the papers after Susan's death, Tim had been getting them multiple times a day for nearly his whole life. The studies on the serum themselves ran until 1985, but according to Michael, Tim was only a participant in his physician's sect of the study for several months from ages six to seven. The rest of his care was managed through steroids and testosterone with no help from cadavers. The mix of hormones did seem to cause aggressive tendencies in Tim, which is no scientific mystery. Even short-term steroid use is correlated with irritability, and imbalances of testosterone are also correlated with aggression. His system was dependent on the concoction, but the side effects weren't the greatest for interpersonal wins. With the constant stream of these synthetic drugs in his system, it's no shock that Tim was combative and unpredictable.

Susan always had a passionate thrust in life, which sometimes manifested in a short fuse. Living with Tim's irrational behavior cut her short fuse even shorter. The two had what newspapers called "an ongoing feud," only mitigated (temporarily, of course) by the Godlike expertise of Dr. Carl Faber. Feud is perhaps an inaccurate word, because both mother and son loved each other, but had inadvertently created a reactionary vacuum. The word "feud" hints at chosen emotional responses and grudges, which it doesn't seem either had the capacity in the 1980s to really engage with. Semantics aside, Susan and Tim were both unhappy and could not rise above the day-to-day frustrations of their situation. In other words, neither saw a way out.

During Tim's trial, there were lots of speculations about which came first: the chicken or the egg. Was Susan mentally ill all along, and *caused* Tim to murder her? Given the presence of these potent drugs in Tim's system at the time of Susan's murder, it is much more likely that the chemical influence they held over him, plus his natural bent as a frustrated, coddled man who suffered greatly from mental and emotional underdevelopment, played a much larger role in his erratic behavior than any measure of environmental subjections. Because of Tim's litany of issues, it was impossible for him to live on his own. Even after Susan's death, he needed residential support and was found to have little capacity for age-appropriate independence. Susan was essentially a caregiver to a medically and emotionally dependent twenty-two-year-old child, but the problem was *she* also needed caregiving in a sense.

Contamination

One of the most hard-hitting blows of Susan's entire life came in 1985 when Tim's specialists gave her devastating news. Doctors told Susan that the injections he had received years before containing the innovative "human growth hormone" to foster his growth, were contaminated with the deadly prion that causes Creutzfeldt-Jakob Disease. A diagnosis of CJD is a fatal condition that causes rapid deterioration of brain cells and eventual death. Tim's specialists did not diagnose him with CJD in 1985, but the medical groups involved in the original study were mandated to contact those who were potentially exposed after several deaths incited an investigation.

In the 1980s, newspapers began to report the disturbing findings of such investigations that the miracle "human growth hormone" had been poisoned all along. While the origin of the disease couldn't be confirmed, it is speculated that one or more of the cadavers used in the study from which to extract pituitary gland enzymes may have been unknowingly infected with CJD and poisoned the whole well, so to speak.

Several participants met an untimely demise years after initially taking the injections because the prion of CJD suddenly activated in their systems several years or even several decades after their initial exposure. In many cases, the adults who suddenly received a diagnosis of CJD barely remembered even taking injections as children, but were still left with the horrid residuals synonymous with a death sentence.

In 1986, the extent of the widespread contamination of the serum wasn't fully known, but many doctors involved in the study were mandated to inform their patients and their parents across the globe that there was a strong likelihood that anyone exposed to even an accidental prick may be at risk of developing CJD. With no cure and virtually no treatment options, parents of children exposed to the serum were simply left in terror to wait for the eventual activation when they would begin exhibiting symptoms of a diseased mind.

When Susan learned the horrible news, her psyche couldn't bear the weight of such a dichotomy of fear and shame. Like so many thousands of other parents, Susan and Michael thought they were truly giving Tim the best shot at a normal, healthy life by approving his participation in the experimental study. Susan's experience wasn't unlike that of the Coussan family, whose son also received injections around the same time as Tim.

Though Tim's specialists were kind enough to personally tell Susan of the contamination once discovered, the Coussans found out their son's fate through impersonal news reports.

"I was devastated," Mrs. Coussan said. "I was angry. I felt like the doctors should have known that I should have been warned. I felt I put my child's life at risk because I was not given complete information." Susan echoed the Coussans in her devastation. Susan's health began to rapidly decline in mid-1986, and it's no wonder. She felt she had been so careful in tending to Tim's needs, perhaps even overly cautious, and yet he was facing a painful and terminal trajectory that could activate any day or night.

After Susan's death, newspapers reported that she suffered a nervous breakdown after learning of Tim's potential for developing CJD. There is no solid evidence of that, but it certainly is plausible. The fear and shame ate her alive, and she wished to God it could be her and not Tim who was facing such a terrible fate.

After the death of their son, the Coussan family established the Parent Council for Growth Normality to offer support for other families like them who lost a loved one to experimental healthcare.

Seclusion

It's hard to know exactly when the term "long-term seclusion" came into the picture, because by all accounts, Susan and Tim both were accustomed to regularly going out in public before and after Michael left until Susan's health declined significantly in late 1986. Each had their own car, and they both regularly went to doctor and therapy appointments. Susan regularly had her hair and nails done at her longtime Beverly Hills salon, Tim went to school, both grocery shopped, and went to the movies. Susan also attended studio events and reunions and had lunch with friends even in the weeks leading up to her murder. But somewhere along the way in media reports, an image of "Norma Desmond" emerged. As an introvert, Susan always claimed to be "really a hermit at heart," but the word "hermit" hints at selective outings while the word "recluse" hints at shuttered darkness and lunacy. It is true that in the few months leading up to her death, her outings significantly decreased because of her bedridden respiratory episodes, but a few months are very different than the decades implied by the newspapers.

Susan was a longtime smoker and reportedly suffered some lung scarring as a result of the whole "too much liquid smoke" thing in *Wasp Woman*, but despite medication management and natural alternatives, breathing could be laborious for days at a time. It's hard to worry about manicuring your lawn when you're struggling for the next breath. Survival can sometimes mimic apathy in appearances, and pinned against physical incapacity and Tim's volatility, surviving was all Susan did in the mid-1980s.

Despite medication, Susan's debilitating asthma and equally debilitating depression and anxiety had her frozen in time. Without another capable adult in the household to make sure general upkeep was taken care of while she was "going through," the combination of her physical and emotional ailments caused many things to fall through the cracks. The accumulation was unfortunately exaggerated tenfold and plastered all over everyone's front page.

It is true by nearly all accounts that Susan's 11,000 square foot showplace on Charmion Lane had fallen into disrepair by the mid-1980s. There were vines looping the gates, Christmas lights left up year-round, slipping doorframes, and an uneven, dying yard in front and back. It is also true that by late 1986, when Susan was killed, she had in fact allowed the house to deteriorate inside as well, with dusty stacks of newspapers, clothes, and painting supplies cluttering nearly every room. As a creative, she was admittedly never concerned with putting things where they belonged in her artist studio because she had her own system and as long as she could find things, it didn't matter if it appeared messy to others. As she began to decline, that philosophy spread to other parts of the house.

It's no crime, of course, to keep a messy house, but given her once vibrant and conscientious spiritedness, the contrast did stand out to family, friends, neighbors, and eventually newspaper readers when the rags reported the condition of the once beautiful hilltop showplace. It certainly was no *Grey Gardens*, but the implication of such sure sold the story, especially in court. Tim's room was reportedly immaculate when responders searched the premises, though he admitted to them later he had intentionally trashed portions of the house before they arrived to make the place look like it had been burglarized. At the crime scene after Susan's death, Deputy Masuda reportedly observed, "It should be noted that the residence was observed in a very unkempt state, which appeared only in part to be due to the ransacking... furniture was overturned and drawers were opened and contents strewn about the residence." Tim's first defense attorney, Chester Leo Smith, said Susan "suffered recurrent mental breakdowns and drew into a reclusive existence into her home...hidden from the outside world [which] exacerbated her son's emotional and developmental retardation."

Paranoia

Like "long-term seclusion," it's also hard to know exactly when the term "paranoid" came into the picture in terms of Susan's mental state, because again, by all accounts, Susan and Tim both regularly met with others and despite some reports, did in fact have friends and family over to their home, however unkempt it may have been. Tim admittedly experienced sways of paranoia himself, as he said in a 2000 *E!* interview that he had psychotic episodes leading up to Susan's death in which he would "go in and out of reality."

Given Susan's history with trauma, it makes sense that she had an almost lifelong hypervigilance that surely increased during her years of severe depression. In 1959, while living in New York alone, Susan had several run-ins with prowlers and alley chases that would make anyone a little edgy about their security. While taking an apartment on the outskirts of Greenwich Village, she described "hand at the window" experiences:

It's in the restaurant and nightclub neighborhood… One night I was on the phone chatting away when I saw the bottom of my window opening up right before my eyes! I stood fixed to the spot wondering how to turn off the light on the other side of the room. I kind of belly-crawled across the room and got to the switch. I heard the prowler jump down and run away.

Susan, who's a fragile little 5'2 and 31, though she doesn't look it, says, 'I've had some other scenes there that are like the Late, Late Show. One night I was watching Bette Davis in 'Elizabeth and Essex' on TV. I had gone to the kitchen to make coffee - and all of a sudden I heard a couple of shots.

Suddenly it occurred to me, 'I don't remember any shooting in 'Elizabeth and Essex.' It became like a private eye thing…. Wondering about those shots…then I heard scuffling…heard a flash…somebody screamed… the police were chasing somebody on my roof!

For a single mother who isn't physically able to defend herself or her special needs son, security, even in Encino, would be a normal concern. There was obsessive mention of "the attack dogs" Susan and Tim had that were reportedly obtained out of "severe paranoia." Although horses were Susan's favorite animal, dogs were easier to maintain inside a mansion. Before Tim was born, Susan was gifted a Yorkshire poodle by her friend Hermione Gingold. She named the little golden-brown pup "Mr. Pie," and he rarely left her arms. After Mr. Pie died shortly after Tim was born, Susan always had a small pack of tiny, fuzzy indoor dogs of various breeds as a part of the family. As Tim's interest in Asian culture developed, he was drawn to the Akita dogs, which have a reputation as loyal protectors of Japanese origin. As puppies, they are fluffy and adorable and reportedly make great snuggle buddies.

As adult dogs, they are exacting and vigilant in protecting their owners and home. Susan allowed Tim to get the dogs, and she hired a trainer to help him learn the art of dog training. All four of the Romans' Akitas were initially trained as puppies, but as he did in most things, Tim lost interest so as adult dogs, their instincts overrode any previous training they had. The dogs lived in the backyard, but had full run of the house when let in. Some of the home's disarray was also reportedly because the dogs essentially lost their minds when Susan was murdered and hordes of strangers entered the home during the police investigation.

Tensions

By 1986, Susan had been officially diagnosed with PTSD, and her once fiery persona was cloaked in a heavy, correlative resignation. In short, she was tired of fighting for Tim and against him. From 1981 until 1986, their codependence flourished without Michael as a present neutralizer. Mother and son were stalemated in resentment, and no one could throw either a lifeline. Tim's resentment toward his mother had a virulence to it that Susan was too weary to engage with by the end of 1986. She had long considered having Tim placed in a facility where he could be cared for by professionals, but she also loved her only child and wanted desperately for him to somehow rise above it all and miraculously be "normal." A facility would not have, in her opinion, given him the best shot at that. So, Tim continued the day-in, day-out love-hate dance around Susan, as her resolve weakened by the hour. As Tim grew into technical adulthood, she gave in to him more and more to avoid further conflict. Constantly pumped full of steroids and testosterone, Tim's aggression often reached scary intensities. Susan found it easier to give in to whatever whim he had than to challenge him, risking escalation.

There were times in Tim's teenage years that his aggression became physical and his mother became his target. Despite the hormone treatment, he was still small for his age, yet taller than she was, and his anger could terrify them both. The times he had physically attacked Susan were either within a delusional state in which he had little awareness, or those times in which their arguments left him feeling like he "had no choice" but to shut her up with physical force. Susan's autopsy noted defensive scratches and bruises on many different areas of her body that were considered unrelated to her cause of death.

Susan was far too protective of Tim to ever seek help with regard to any degree of physical abuse he may have perpetrated. Further, in the 1970s and 1980s, resources for victims of domestic violence were not plentiful, especially for women who were victims of their children's assaults. With Susan's complex history of sexual and physical abuse, it is not far-fetched to think she would compartmentalize the difficulties between her and Tim even when they escalated to dangerous levels of violence. In her over-protection of Tim, she excused his outbursts as she excused everything else in the spirit of self-preservation.

The first-ever empirical study on children abusing their parents was conducted in 1957 by researchers Sears, Maccoby, and Levin. Sears et al. referred to the "new" type of domestic violence as "battered parent syndrome." Domestic violence usually refers to physical, sexual, or psychological violence between intimate partners, but in more recent years, the study of child-to-parent violence (CPV) has been increasingly recognized as another means individuals (children) may use to gain and/or maintain control over another person (their parent).

Susan, like so many victims of CPV, lived in a cage of shame over Tim's violent outbursts. She had tried to help him channel his lifelong tendencies with martial arts courses and psychotherapy, but nothing seemed to decrease his boiling point. Susan felt like she had somehow "caused" Tim's behavior, and her support system enabled that belief in failing to address Tim's behavior as *his own behavior* separate from his mother's identity and decisions.

Any abuse Tim perpetuated on Susan, her guilt and shame in believing she deserved it because of some inadequacy on her part in mothering Tim kept her quiet about his behavior. The resounding question that hurt almost as much as Tim's attacks was: "What kind of mother am I that I raised a child that can do this to me?"

Feminist author Betty Friedan said in her revolutionary book *The Feminine Mystique* (1963):

[It is] safer to take it out on his wife and his

mother than to recognize a failure in himself or in the sacred American way of life.

Because of her early years of abuse and neglect, it was more familiar to Susan to suffer in silence with Tim in their hilltop mansion than to blow the whistle on the violence occurring behind closed doors, but the fear of what kind of "help" she might find on the other side of whistle-blowing terrified her as much as the pounding of his fists.

There didn't seem to be a pattern to Tim's triggers. Sometimes he was calm, rational, and easy to get along with. At other times, he was a madman with blood in his eyes. He would turn on Susan in a millisecond with sudden verbal attacks of name-calling and threats that would escalate to shoves, slaps, and punches. His abuse hurt terribly, and his Jekyll and Hyde pace made her a hypervigilant nerve ending.

Susan, like many parents of abusive children, would have had the burden of convincing police she was truly the victim of abuse, which would have been difficult given the time period and limited scope of awareness on "battered parent syndrome" in the 1980s. Admitting to herself that she was a victim of such was difficult enough, but then convincing the authorities was an entirely different kind of complication. The risk of the authorities not believing her was as heavy as Tim's hand.

The most probable means of help Susan may have received (assuming she was believed) would have been Tim's physical removal from the home—temporarily or permanently. If she phoned the police during one of his attacks, they would have most likely arrested Tim. An arrest for him may or may not have resulted in his institutionalization within either the cogs of the judicial or mental health systems, and Susan would have rather cut off her right arm than have Tim taken from their home by some regulatory entity.

No matter how unmanageable Tim's behavior, Susan simply couldn't stand the thought of watching strangers take him away into the systemic abyss, much like the day the state of Massachusetts tore her mother Muriel from their Dorchester home with one hand, leaving Susan to fall into the state's other hand of foster care. The scene of being physically dragged from the clutches of her mother and home was emblazoned in Susan's memory for her lifetime, and the horrible potential for reenactment was something she was constantly aware of with Tim.

Because of the terrible knowledge both Susan and Tim carried that the CJD lay dormant in his cells and could virtually activate unprovoked at any minute, Susan didn't know how much longer Tim had in his earthly existence. To think of Tim spending his last weeks or months in a cold jail or sanatorium cell was too much for her to bear. The resignation Susan had fallen into in the last few years of her life was far more layered than the "Norma Desmond" portrait the press and defense painted—she was, in her eyes, protecting Tim even if it cost Susan her own safety.

The more his outbursts escalated, the further into resignation she fell. The Romans had experts from nearly every field involved in their situation on one level or another, yet even as a grown adult, Susan found herself a child again—chained as a prisoner in her own home.

The pain and the shame kept her locked in silence, for what entity would help her without victim-blaming and mother-blaming more than they already had? The fear of those dreaded responses has bolted many victims' mouths shut since the beginning of time, so every day was a repeat of the one before, existing in sheer survival mode. She placated, humored, and excused in place of seeking a way out. It's easy now to say, "If only she had…" But by the time Tim's abuse had reached alarming proportions, Susan Cabot Roman was tired. She had weathered nearly sixty years of battles, and she was tired of the fight.

Tim's weak sense of self and exaggerated, steroid-influenced emotions worked to perpetuate a latent anger that never seemed to die. Everything he did seemed only to fuel the fire. His resolve caved daily to the bullies at school. What he never had the nerve to do to them, he felt free to do to his mother.

Chapter Seven
Ninjas & Blunt Force Trauma

"Don't you see now that I could have poisoned you a hundred times had I been able to live without you."

— Cleopatra

Around 8:30pm on December 10, 1986, Tim angrily paced in his room intermittently lifting barbells, seeking relief from the anger that nearly burned him alive. The worn weightlifting equipment was usually an effective outlet after quarrels with his mother, but as he furiously paced and shakily lifted that night, his anger only intensified. His mind raced with replays of the argument he had with Susan earlier in the evening, after which he escaped to his room behind a familiar slam of his door.

Susan had been bedridden with severe asthma symptoms and fatigue for several days, and that evening, the two had been lying in her master bed together watching TV when Tim's temper flared. It was a typical rift for the two caused by everything and nothing at all.

His room was like a ninja haven in offering both escape and catharsis. Since middle school, Tim had been obsessed with Bruce Lee films and knew the films' entire scripts by heart. He obsessively acted out Lee's choreography in addition to his own martial arts class teachings presumably in an effort to establish his own power over his situation. His medical conditions, his lifelong bullies, and his co-dependent dance with his mother left him feeling perpetually helpless.

The day of Susan's death, Tim had attended his college classes as usual. There was the routine, end-of-the-semester push before pre-holiday finals, and he had been cramming at the library with intermittent dragon-drawing breaks before coming home.

While Tim was at school that day, Susan allegedly had another one of her frequent psychotherapy sessions with Dr. Carl Faber. For over two decades, Faber had set himself up as Susan's armchair savior. He was dynamic, understanding, and affirming. He seemed to know what she was thinking and could often finish her sentences, leaving her in sheer worship of the man and his expertise. She was sure he was a prophet. She never made *any* decision without first consulting him.

Faber testified at Tim's trial, saying upon their last session Susan had tearfully admitted to him something she never intended to tell anyone. She said if it weren't for Tim, she would kill herself. Her reason for living was her son, and she confessed she was "tired and wanted to go, and if it wasn't for Timothy, I would." Dr. Faber noted Susan was in "tremendous despair," but capable of "irrational actions" in his witness stand sympathies toward Tim, suggesting Susan, in fact, had more to do with her own murder than Tim did.

The truth is, Susan did *not* go see Dr. Faber the day of her death. Her last session with him had been several days before December 10. She was too ill on the 10th to do much of anything and spent most of the day and night in bed.

***

Around 8:30pm on December 10, 1986, Susan tossed and turned. No matter how she positioned herself, she couldn't escape the feeling of suffocation. She had used and overused her inhalers that day, but nothing seemed to help. She felt the weight of an anvil on her chest and every breath was a gasp. She had intermittent asthma attacks since childhood, but over the last several years her lungs seemed to be shutting down one lobe at a time. At fifty-nine Susan's respiratory system was frail and her energy tanked quickly, often causing her to be bedridden for days at a time. Her mind raced with replays of the spat she had with Tim earlier in the evening, after which he escaped to his room with a familiar slam of his door. After Tim had arrived home from college that afternoon, the two had dinner and were lying in her master bed together watching TV when he became enraged.

Susan let the memories of his angry words trickle away as she tried to mentally follow the breathing regimen she had held tightly to for years, given by a former analyst:

There is nothing like deep breathing to fill your system with oxygen and to revitalize the bloodstream. Stand before an open window and exhale so as to rid your lungs of stale breath. When you think they are empty, give an extra exhalation to flatten them. Then start to breathe deeply and slowly, and if you find yourself yawning after this, it's a good sign that you have broken the tension and are many degrees more relaxed.

It was a typical rift for the two caused by everything and nothing at all. Susan loved Tim deeply and often reminded him how much she had lovingly sacrificed for him, but there was a wall of thorns between them that seemed to grow higher and higher as he aged. She knew others, including Tim, saw her as overbearing and too protective, but they simply didn't understand her plight as the long-suffering single mother. If she didn't protect Tim, who would?

Part of the madness of Susan and Tim's feuding pattern was in how quickly he seemed to turn on her after an innocent comment or suggestion that was always, according to her, made in his best interest. He lashed out at her questions of interest about his school day, friends, and classes. Their accumulating arguments hadn't caused Susan to love Tim any less, but after years of feeling she had altogether lost him, she felt a haunting resignation about the future of nearly everything.

Finally, around 9:00pm on the night of December 10, Susan welcomed her next dose of the bronchodilator Theophylline she was prescribed. After taking it, she switched positions and began finding some relief from the anvil on her chest. As counterintuitive as it seemed, her doctor had told her lying on her stomach would often take some of the pressure off the diaphragm, encouraging "belly breathing," and could help decrease symptoms of an attack. Susan often used it as a last resort in order to sleep because it is never particularly comfortable having your face mashed into the mattress just to breathe. She started to feel calmer, soon her breathing came more easily, and she fell off into the black of sleep.

***

Tim was annoyed at his mother's comment while the two had been watching TV. His annoyance soon turned to rage. Then the rage consumed him until it became his entire temporary existence. He started to sweat as he paced his room faster and faster. He thought of her sleeping soundly while he was left to deal with such furor on his own. He thought of tearing down curtains, breaking his windows, storming into her room and letting her have a second round, but nothing he thought of seemed to bring relief. Whatever he did, he would have to pay the price for, and his tomorrows were never any better than his yesterdays, so even if this particular argument was resolved, a different one would undoubtedly come up the next day.

In his manic pacing, finally something in him let loose as his vision zeroed in on a pair of ten-pound barbells. He calculatingly picked one up in an angry clinch. He had fantasies of using his martial arts training on his mother in the thick of her lectures. He often fantasized about what it would be like to tower over her during one of her critiques and belt her until she stopped.

As he held the steel of the barbell, an awful impulse possessed him. Suddenly, the weight in his hand was all he could think about. The clock showed 9:30pm. He knew his mother was asleep. With the weight in his sweating hand, he crept down the corridor to her room. She kept her door closed after retiring in the evenings, so he listened quietly outside for several seconds. Hearing nothing, he gently turned the knob and nudged the door open. The room was dark, but he saw her slender figure lying motionless across the bed, face down. Her back was rhythmically rising and falling in sound sleep. She wore only a purple, V-necked negligée. In a twisted reenactment of her days in foster care, Tim would be the last slinking figure with devilish intentions to creep into her bedroom while she slept.

In the silence, Tim hovered over Susan for several seconds, watching the rise and fall of her back. There lay the woman who birthed him, cooed to him as a baby, softly sang him to sleep so many nights, spoke tenderly to him about how wrong the bullies at school were, and wiped his bloody nose from another locker-room incident. There also lay the woman who, in his opinion, had limited him, dominated him, deprived him of "normalcy," criticized him, and quarreled so uncompromisingly. He hated her. He hated what she had done to him, to their house, to Michael, to herself. He noticed a linen towel near the bed. In his premeditation, he gently draped the linen over the back of her head as she slept. His mind was an abyss of anger as he drew the barbell back over his shoulder. In one angry motion, Tim slammed the end of the weight down on the back of his mother's head. She let out a whimper that was more involuntary than anything, and he struck her again. And again. And again. After several blows, and with nothing else tangible left of Susan's head and face, it was over.

Everything was over. She was dead. Tim heard only his own heavy breathing and the sound of her blood dripping from the headboard, and suddenly, perhaps for the first time in his life, he felt calm.

Everything in Susan's bedroom, including Tim, was spattered with blood and bits of brain matter from floor to ceiling. In seeing the tissue shards of her head splayed across the bed, Tim found a second clean red linen and covered the bloody remnants of what was intact just seconds before.

Standing alone in the silence, breathless but filled with relief, Tim called the police. "911, what's your emergency?" asked the dispatcher's voice on the other end of the phone. "My mother. She's dead," Tim calmly stated.

Tim had caught his breath by the time paramedics and police arrived, and they found him "calm and cool." John Beiner and his partner, Robert Gocke, with the Los Angeles Fire Department were the first to respond. It took over six hours before they could access Susan's bedroom because the

Akitas did their job of keeping people out a little too well. Tim gave Los Angeles Police Detective Joe Diglio and his team permission to search the home, but the four dogs did not. There was a lot of dead space for the police as they waited for animal control to seize the dogs. That gave police plenty of time to note the dying plants surrounding the front steps, peeling paint, and chipped steps. For all the disrepair Diglio had noticed upon his outside inspection of the home, the inside was much more unsettling. Diglio and his men felt like they were walking onto a horror movie set with cobwebs and mildew decorating the front stoop. When they entered the front foyer, they reportedly found a bizarre hoarder's maze difficult to navigate.

While waiting on animal control, Tim initially told responders that "Latino ninjas" had broken into their home. Then he claimed it was just one "Japanese ninja" who had attacked him, beat Susan, and made off with $70,000. He said he went to bed around 9:30pm but couldn't sleep and went to the kitchen for a snack around 10:00pm. There he encountered the "ninja intruder" who supposedly stabbed him in the arm before rendering him unconscious with a blow to the head. About half an hour later, he awoke confused and immediately dialed 911.

Ninja Attacks

While Tim had a longstanding fascination with Asian culture and ninjas, in the mid-1980s, newspapers reported a nationwide string of killings that all had a peculiar similarity: the killers were clad in black ninja attire. One of the first and perhaps most well-known of the "ninja murders" was also dubbed the "Yom Kippur Murders." On September 25, 1985, in West Los Angeles, Gerald and Vera Woodman were attacked in their home just after returning from a celebration of the Jewish holiday Yom Kippur, or "The Day of Atonement." The couple was found in their home shot to death, though with nothing having been taken from their home, the motive wasn't readily clear. The crime investigation eventually led police to the couple's two sons, Neil and Stewart Woodman, who confessed to hiring two men to dress in ninja suits and murder their parents so they could collect on their life insurance policies.

After the Yom Kippur murders, many copycat killings cascaded over California and other states. *The Philadelphia Inquirer*'s 1987 headline reads: Growing cult of ninja imitators brings a rise in crime." Several other seemingly random attacks by assailants dressed in ninja attire made headlines in the 1980s. The oddest account was perhaps that of the two teenagers dressed as ninjas who held actress Penny Marshall hostage in her Hollywood home.

Of all the warrior reports, the University of Kentucky gunman hit a little too close to home to Susan — even all the way in sunny California.

On the day Susan was murdered, a series of other killings took place at the hands of a ninja in central Kentucky, more than two thousand miles away. A former University employee, Ulysses Davis, III, opened fire on campus after he claimed to be slighted by the institution. Davis wounded two men during his attack and kept police and the entire campus in a stalemate for nearly eleven hours.

Ninjas were in the forefront of every newspaper reader's mind in the 1980s, and police were certainly aware of the peculiar crime fad. So, when Tim claimed a ninja broke into the Romans' home and killed his mother, it wasn't quite the random accusation it may sound like today.

Susan and Tim's longtime psychologist, Dr. Carl Faber, was interviewed about the emergence of the ninja phenomenon prior to Susan's murder. *The Los Angeles Times* reporter Arnold Shapiro wrote:

> *Although the Los Angeles Police Department says Los Angeles is the safest big city in the country, many Southern California residents fear being raped, robbed, mugged, or murdered. People are enrolling in self-defense courses in record numbers, even though most of them have never experienced personal violence. Dr. Carl Faber, a clinical psychologist, attributes the rising interest in martial arts to anxiety. 'People feel they can't rely on police protection,' he explains, and they can't rely on the aggressor to fight fairly and be rational. For instance, he might be a desperate heroin addict. So they have to escalate their own abilities to deal, by*

themselves, with situations that have no fairness boundaries.' Dr. Faber also feels that what is 'Eastern' is interesting right now = 'there's still a newness to the Oriental arts.'

Despite the heightened awareness of ninja attacks and the trend of martial arts training to discourage those attacks, the police were naturally suspicious of Tim's story from the minute they arrived on the scene. His demeanor was reportedly "peculiar," and nothing he relayed seemed to add up. There was no sign of forced entry, and an intruder surely couldn't have gotten past the ferocious dogs. Deputy Masuda noted:

Four dogs also resided at the location, the dogs were locked in an anteroom upon my arrival. An attempt had been made earlier in the morning to have Los Angeles Animal Control officers remove the dogs. The animals proved to be too vicious to be removed by animal control officers and remained locked in a room during the investigation. The dogs had been placed in the anteroom by Timothy Roman.

Another red flag among the dozens of responders noticed was that Tim had no wounds consistent with his story of an attacker. He did, in fact, have a surface cut on his arm and "slight bruise" on his forehead, but neither sufficiently corresponded with the "ninja attack" story.

Detective Joe Diglio noted in his investigative report:

...when Timothy Roman was questioned about the incident, his statements became increasingly inconsistent. Mr. Roman reportedly told police that he heard his mother being 'hit with a hammer,' which woke him at approximately 2130 hours on the evening of the incident.

Tim's odd, conflicting accounts of what happened that night were all over the place, but once the dogs were apprehended and police had access to the home, they finally put the puzzle pieces together.

In the dark, early hours of December 11, police cautiously wove through the entirety of the home, one room at a time. With every room came an additional layer to their confusion as they were met with piles of cigarette butts, stacks of newspapers, strewn food wrappers, crumpled mail, and mounds of clothes. After rounding the doorframe of the master bedroom upstairs, Gocke found himself in a bloodbath. Lying across the king-sized master bed was the lifeless remains of B-movie queen Susan Cabot Roman.

The crime scene was nearly as strange as Tim's demeanor. With Susan's brain matter clubbed across the mattress and headboard, blunt force trauma was obvious. Arches of blood dotted with bits of black hair were splattered across her bedroom mirror and ceiling, sliding down together into dried pools on the floor. Gocke noted the rest of her body was in visibly "good" condition. Her face and her teeth having been buried in the mattress appeared almost untouched, which was disturbing by itself, making her a headless, bloody form in a purple negligée. Gocke also noted a "red, blood-stained cloth" had been placed over where her head had been.

> *[We] observed the decedent lying prone and [sic] the bed in her bedroom. The decedent's head was pointed toward a mirror on the wall of the bedroom. She was lying across the bed, side to side, her feet were hanging over the one side, her head over the other. A moderate amount of blood was observed, on the numerous objects covering the bedroom floor, under the decedent's head... The head of the decedent was covered with a blanket or piece of bed linen. There were 'tool' marks noted in the bed linen. Blood splatters were noted on the mirror, bed and ceiling of the decedent's bedroom. The blood splatters appeared consistent with having been flung upon the area by the instrument used by the suspect, as the decedent appeared to have had her head covered during the entire bludgeoning incident.*

Police subsequently searched Tim's room and found the murder weapon: a ten-pound barbell hidden in a box of "Bold 3" laundry detergent in the bottom of his hamper. At trial, that was one of the most damning pieces of evidence against him because it contradicted the "sudden rage defense," since he apparently had time and brain enough to hide the weapon after striking her. Police and eventually the jury decided that Tim's matricide was at least partially premeditated—inasmuch as he was mentally capable.

Responders initially thought Tim was a young preteen and were shocked to learn he was actually twenty-two. With his clear complexioned baby face and short stature, Tim presented as a confused, emotionless child when he answered the door. It was clear something was off with him, but just *what* wasn't revealed until his first trial. Along with his dwarfism, his system was overrun with the synthetic concoction of steroids and testosterone.

Responders didn't know it at the time, but they were interviewing an emotionally disturbed, steroid-stuffed guy with *major* mom issues, so no wonder something seemed off.

Though the official account of December 10 changed several times throughout the course of initial proceedings, Tim ultimately said he and his mother had been in another one of their acidic arguments, and she tried to attack him with a scalpel and a barbell. He claimed his matricide was simply self-defense, both figuratively, given their nefarious situation, and literally given her alleged aggression toward him that evening. Susan was found to have no defensive wounds related to her death, and her autopsy revealed she was, in fact, asleep at the time of her murder.

Tim later testified that Susan had been in bed with severe asthma attacks for several days. That night, Tim said she was having an "extreme psychotic episode" with "screaming, calling for her mother, talking to herself." He said, "I thought I'd better get help..... Then she started saying, 'Who are you?'" He claimed he picked up the phone to call for paramedics when she came at him with a scalpel in one hand and a barbell in the other. She supposedly used the scalpel in gardening, and the barbell to keep in shape, though neither would have been particularly useful to someone in failing health. "I was trying to push her away... just to get out of that room," he said, and then things went blank. The next thing he knew, his mother was dead.

Susan's autopsy wasn't as vague as Tim's "things went blank" story. The report reads: "The decedent has been massively and multiply bludgeoned to the back region of the head…OPINION: Susan Roman, a 59-year-old White female, died of bludgeoning head injuries. Homicide."

Tim was known to have psychotic episodes, not Susan. Her autopsy confirms she was suffering from severe respiratory inflammation at the time of her death, and the only substances found in her system were prescribed asthma medications. The medical examiner noted she was evidently suffering from a cold or the flu at the time of death.

She also had multiple defense wounds on several areas of her body that were marked as unrelated to her cause of death. Many of the defense wounds were considered products of prior incidents, presumably *with* Tim. Her autopsy noted prior defensive wounds on her right hand, right forearm, right wrist, upper back, left hip, and inner thighs. This litany of previous injuries brings up the question of domestic violence, with Tim as the only potential able-bodied perpetrator. In the condition reflected in her autopsy, it is difficult to believe she would have been able-bodied enough to engage with Tim in any type of verbal altercation, much less a physical one.

The evidence of injury directly related to Susan's cause of death was specified in her autopsy report:

Brief history: A 59-year-old Caucasian female actress found bludgeoned, prone on bed in nightgown at her residence about 2246 hours (time of parmedics [sic] arrival) and pronounced dead at 2250 hours of 12/10/86, after her son called paramedics. Son claimed a 'burglar' was responsible, however, police, after questioning son, have him as suspect in custody. Evidence of injury: The decedent has been massively and multiply bludgeoned to the back region of her head. Present in the mid to mid-right occipital scalp, as diagramed on Form 20-F, and photographed, is a gaping irregular, over 4x3 inch lacerated jagged scalp defect in which can be seen multiple comminuted fragments of the shattered posterior region of the skull, as well as fragments of damaged brain and dura. Radiating upwards from this main defect is a 3-inch incontinuity radiating laceration. On the left upper occipital to left posterior parietal skull there is a roughly vertical somewhat irregular full thickness 2-inch laceration to the galea. On the upper mid occipital scalp just above the major defect is an approximately 1-inch full thickness laceration. On the right upper occipital area there is a small 1/2 inch irregular nearly full thickness laceration. On the right posteriormost temporal to anterosuperior occipital scalp there is a roughly vertically oriented 5/8 inch in height fairly smooth edged laceration showing some bridging of tissue strands in its depth, and extending to the galea. Just under the above-mentioned 5/8 inch laceration is a 1/4 x 3/8 inch nearly full thickness laceration, irregular, and showing bridging of tissue strands in its depth. In the right posterolateral lower occipital area behind the mastoid region is a 3/4 x 1/2 inch full thickness laceration associated with comminuted fracturing underlying it. On the left upper posterior parietal scalp there is a 1-1/8 x 1/2 inch nearly fully thickness irregular laceration to the galea. The posterior region of the skull including most of the occiput is literally shattered into multiple comminuted fragments and multiple fragments have been pushed into the lacerated dura and brain substance. Fracturing of the skull is diagramed on Form 20-G, and includes the major occipital defect, which measures about 4 x 3 inches, and also radiating fractures into the right posterior parietal bone, and radiating basal fractures to the foramen magnum. There is a nondisplaced slight fracture on the right orbital roof, apparently due to transmission of forces of the bludgeoning to the orbital roof through the brain substance. The inner portion of the right eye area shows a focus of purplish ecchymosis related to this orbital fracture. Blood is present in the nose and ear canals related to basal skull fracturing. As diagrammed on Form 20-D, the brain is massively injured by the bludgeoning and there are lacerations and disruptions of cerebral substance in the occipital poles bilaterally, especially on the right, and in the posterior aspects of the cerebellar lobes there are also lacerations. The brain shows 1+ to 2+ edema overall and shows a global film of bright red subarachnoid hemorrhage. As noted previously, multiple comminuted fragments of the occipital bone have been pushed into the posterior region of the brain. As diagramed on Form 20, present on the right upper lateral back near the posterior right shoulder region there is a superficial dark red 5/8 x

3/8 inch abrasion. On the upper mid back there are two (2) parallel similar 1/4 inch superficial scratch-type abrasions. On the dorsal aspect of the decedent's right forearm, there is a roughly rectangularly shaped 1-1/8 x 3/8 inch dark red abrasion, possibly a defensive injury. On the dorsal aspect of the decedent's right distal forearm near the wrist, radial aspect, there is a 3/4 inch purplish recent-appearing contusion, possibly defensive. On the dorsum of the decedent's right hand there are purplish recent-appearing defensive-type contusions including purplish ecchymosis of the proximal dorsal portion of the right little finger, a similar purplish contusion ecchymosis of the proximal portion of the right ring finger, and a faint 1/2 inch area of contusion ecchymosis, purplish of the dorsal radial aspect of the right hand near the base of the first finger. There is slight abrasion of the contusion injury of the ring finger. The decedent's left lateral posterior hip area just lateral to the left buttock shows two (2) faint apparently recent patchy areas of contusion, each measuring about 2-1/2 x 1 inch. There are several clearly old minor bruises on the right thigh and left knee, which will be described later in the report.

To summarize in layman's terms: the damage was bad. Really, really bad. I'm certainly no forensic expert, but the extent of damage described in Susan's autopsy can't be attributed to the "little self-defense incident" Tim initially reported. And the prosecution didn't think so either.

This was no knock over the head in an attempt to flee a confrontation, as Tim eventually described in court. The autopsy says it all. This was deliberate, diabolical brutality of inconceivable proportions. In attempting to cover up such barbarism, Tim panicked, lied, and hid the murder weapon. In detectives' initial investigations, premeditation was also noted.

Detective Diglio's initial incident report reads as follows:

On 12-10-86, Timothy Roman, contacted the Los Angeles City Fire Department and Police Department, to report the entry of a 'burglar' into the residence, described above, which he shared with his mother. Mr. Roman reported injuries to himself and that he also believed that his mother was injured. Los Angeles City Fire Department paramedics responded to the location and found the decedent dead in her bedroom. Death was pronounced at 2250 by RA51. Mr. Roman told paramedics that the incident occurred at approximately 2130 hours on the same date. Paramedics questioned the son, Timothy Roman, as to the length of time it took him to call for assistance, the initial alarm was at 2240 hours. Mr. Roman told paramedics that during his altercation with the suspect, he was knocked unconscious. Paramedics examined Mr. Roman and found him to have superficial wounds to the arm, torso, and head. Paramedics reported to police that the trauma to the head of Timothy Roman did not appear serious enough to cause unconsciousness.

***

As dawn approached, the coroner carried Susan's body from the home on a stretcher with the flash of emergency lights rebounding off the home's dingy white exterior. The tired estate sat darkened and hollow as the bagged remains of its former owner were loaded into the back of the coroner's vehicle. Susan and her home were both once beautiful, bright figures of grandeur and now both were decomposing corpses. Timothy Scott Roman, twenty-two, was arrested for the murder of Susan Cabot Roman, fifty-nine. After police read him his rights, he tearfully shouted with the voice of a pre-pubescent boy: "I *loved* her!" Tim was arrested, but Susan was ultimately the one who was tried and convicted for her own murder.

Chapter Eight
The Trial of Susan Cabot Roman

"Probably the best things I remember about her is that she was a very sweet person."

— Timothy Scott Roman

"There was some type of argument, but he's not telling us what it was," Diglio said. After initial questioning and thorough crime scene scour, Diglio also indicated there was evidence of premeditation. After Tim was taken into custody, he was found upon examination to have all kinds of hormonal imbalances, including "crazy high" thyroid levels. Though he was later found competent enough to stand trial, severe "unspecified" mental and physical developmental delays were noted in his evaluation, along with the endocrinal wreckage of his body.

Tim was questioned for over ninety minutes by West Valley detectives, during which he never really "broke." He did, however, become combative during the interview, which initially didn't help his whole "meek and mild victim" defense when they later played the tape in court. He was looking at twenty-five years to life and held without bail.

Evidentially

The cards were stacked against Tim from the beginning, of course, though he prolonged the inevitable as long as he could with stories of ninjas and blackouts. The evidence was damning, and so were his contradictory accounts of how his mother met her demise.

Tim eventually confessed to killing Susan after they found the weapons he "hid" in the laundry detergent box.

With his tearful confession, his defense went straight for the "Norma Desmond" angle.

Despite Tim's stunted cognitive functioning, one of the most damning pieces of evidence that was apparently glossed over in his second and final trial was his attempt to hide the weapon he used to kill his mother. The defense gave reason after reason for why Tim should be dealt with particularly mercifully because of his limitations, yet investigators found both the barbell he used to beat Susan and the scalpel that she allegedly came after him with in a box of laundry detergent. When questioned about hiding the items, Tim said he panicked and hid them because he didn't think anyone would believe him that his mother tried to attack him with both items. Deputy District Attorney Bradford E. Stone said, "If he flamed out, how do you explain that the murder weapon got from his bedroom to hers, where she was beaten to death? That takes some degree of thinking and planning."

Initially, Judge Raymond Mireles disqualified himself from the case, and Judge Richard Kolostian heard Tim's first trial in Van Nuys. He denied Tim and his counsel's motion to plead "not guilty by reason of developmental disability," partly because Tim was found competent enough to stand trial. Tim's original defense attorney, Chester Leo Smith, pushed a psychological defense. He argued Tim "suffered because of an overprotective, disturbed mother and a severe growth deficiency that made him dependent on strong medications with dangerous side effects." There was, however, a conflict of interest at play with Smith because he and Susan had been friends for more than three decades. She used his services as a real estate attorney for her properties and investments, as well as filing for divorce against Michael in 1981. Instead of risking repercussions over the technicality, Smith reportedly had a heart attack instead. His absence resulted in a mistrial in May 1989.

There were rumors that Smith wanted to benefit from the fortune Tim inherited from Susan's death, and if he helped Tim get off with a light sentence, he could retire in luxury. That was never substantiated, of course, but it is odd that such a longtime friend of Susan's would push so hard for her conviction of her own murder. The other side of the point, however, is that perhaps Smith was, in fact, an altruistic-blooded man who perhaps thought he was honoring Susan's memory and love for Tim by helping him. Whatever Smith's motivations were, he was replaced with public defenders who knew a little more about criminal law than Smith did as a real estate attorney.

Tim was appointed defense attorneys Richard P. Lasting and Michael V. White by Judge Darlene Schempp for the second trial. While they fiddled with the "self-defense" routine, it just couldn't hold water given Susan's weakened state at the time of her death. Her autopsy was clear that she was in poor health, suffering from either the flu or a cold, and also sound asleep when the first blow came.

The Los Angeles Times reported:

Taking the witness stand in his own defense for the first time Thursday, Timothy Scott Roman, tearfully testified that his mother, actress Susan Cabot, attacked him with a barbell and a scalpel the night she was found bludgeoned to death in her Encino home. Roman, dressed in a neat gray pinstripe suit, spoke softly as he described finding his mother dead in her room. But, he said, he does not remember killing her, as prosecutors allege.

Lasting and White's overall defense for Tim was similar to the one Smith had advised Tim on: they never disputed Tim killed Susan, but they "contended that Cabot provoked the killing with aggressive, irrational behavior and that Roman's actions were caused by hormones and drugs he took because he did not have a pituitary gland."

Newspapers went into great detail about how court records supposedly reflected Susan's usage of Tim's injections in order to recapture her youth. The only thing anyone could point to as "evidence" of her having self-injected the serum was her "perfect, wrinkle-free skin." Well, that and the whole "she played a character in a movie who did that" thing. It made a great story, and reporters reasoned that because she had no wrinkles, she must have just thrown all sense out of the window and taken her child's experimental injections that had nothing whatsoever to do with a youthful appearance. As a matter of fact, Tim was technically taking the drug for the opposite effect; growth has rarely been synonymous with youth. Incidentally, Susan's autopsy reported "no chronic needle track scars."

Painting Susan's Portrait

For all the painting Susan did in her life, it was Tim's defense team that painted over the legacy she had built over fifty-nine years before her brutal murder. The trials of the "dwarf" who slayed his B-movie queen mother were electric. Newspapers and tabloids stayed in printing frenzies with proceedings updates and speculations tied to Susan's career and reports of the case's spooky particulars like the connection between her life and her film work, the luxurious squalor mother and son reportedly lived in, and of course the identity of Tim's *real* father. It became a Hollywood sensation story, not half as concerned with facts, as it was the mosaic of a deranged villainess caught in a slow, sad decline provoking her medically complicated, dwarfed son to murder. Proceedings echoed by the press painted Susan as a washed-up "Norma Desmond," insane with perpetual rage and paranoia, while Tim was the medically fragile captive driven to slaughter in contextual self-defense. Susan was put on trial for her own murder because she allegedly "yelled sometimes," according to him.

Tim's first defense attorney (and Susan's former close friend), Chester Leo Smith, was quoted during proceedings: "In focusing on Roman's mother's fragile mental condition, her unkempt home and her authorization of controversial drugs for her son, the defense intends to show that she may have contributed to her own death."

It was a clear case of victim-blaming all the way around. In her work *Victim-Blaming: A New Term for an Old Trend*, Julia Churchill Schoellkopf (2012) asserts this based on her study of the victim-blaming phenomenon:

> *Victim-blaming is a phenomenon that has been happening since at least the beginning of recorded history but has only recently been identified as a dynamic used to empower the criminal and maintain the status quo.*

> *Victim-blaming is perpetuated by sexism, the Just World Theory, cognitive biases, and the theories of self-blame. Victim-blaming occurs...when the victim of a crime or abuse is held partly or entirely responsible for the actions committed against them. In other words, the victims are held accountable for the maltreatment they have been subjected to. Perpetrators of crimes for which they blame the victim commonly enjoy a privileged social status opposite the victim, and their blame typically involves use of stereotypical negative words.*

The victim-blaming in the case of Susan Cabot Roman wasn't some conspiracy against her in particular, it was simply an overarching societal tendency that happened to bleed over into the judicial system, especially during the era of the 1980s and 1990s and before. The prejudice against women who operated outside of conventional gender roles as perhaps single, working mothers like Susan who engaged with their children from a dual platform as both mother and father was and is a thorny reality that has yet to be fully abolished.

In 1942, writer Philip Wylie infamously coined the term "momism" in his best-selling, disturbingly misogynistic book *Generation of Vipers*. "Momism" was used to describe what he claimed was an epidemic of mothers who fostered an "excessive attachment to, or domination over" their children (primarily their sons). Wiley asserted that momism was a threat to the moral fiber of America on par with communism. In 1945, psychiatrist Edward Strecker picked up where Wiley's book left off and argued that the 2.5 million men rejected or discharged from the Army as unfit during World War II were the product of overly protective mothers, or "momism" as it were.

Certainly, all parents, whether male or female, are generally responsible for the type of environment they create for their children to grow up within, but mother-blaming is far beyond that. Mother-blaming is the unfair and unrealistic layer added to the basic responsibility every parent has to competently care for and love their child. Mother-blaming is a misogynistically driven tendency to first point the finger at the mother for her assumed contribution to their child's negative outcome as an adult. Pointing the finger in this context isn't referring to obvious abuse/neglect dynamics, but ancillary things like "if you're a poorly adjusted adult, your mother must have been promiscuous or overbearing or frigid."

Feminist author Betty Friedan said in *The Feminine Mystique* (1963): Under the Freudian microscope… it was suddenly discovered that the mother could be blamed for almost anything. In every case history of a troubled child… could be found a mother … A rejecting, overprotecting, dominating mother. World War II revealed that millions of American men were psychologically incapable of facing the shock of war, of facing life away from their 'moms'. Clearly something was 'wrong' with American women.

There are trillions of examples of society's historical bent toward mother-blaming from the beginning of time until today in the 2020s within all fields. Some of the most cringey examples came from the field of psychology itself: In the 1940s, Austrian psychiatrist Leo Kanner claimed to discover the causation of autism: mothers. Kanner coined the term "refrigerator mother" to describe mothers who were cold and distant in their parenting style, which he asserted traumatized children so thoroughly that they retreated into an autistic state. Psychiatrist Frieda Fromm-Reichman developed a similar theory in the 1950s that like autism, schizophrenia was caused by "schizophrenogenic mothers." Fromm-Reichman (1948) said, "The schizophrenic is painfully distrustful and resentful of other people, due to the severe early warp and rejection he encountered in important people of his infancy and childhood, as a rule, mainly in a schizophrenogenic mother." These examples of mother-blaming may seem outrageous and very dated, because of course we now know mothers do not "cause" neurobiological conditions such as autism or schizophrenia, but the concept of "mother-is-to-blame" is still deeply embedded in society's functionalism.

In entertainment, we see similar themes of "wherever there's misery, there's a mom" from Hitchcock's *Psycho* to *Mommie Dearest* to more recent productions such as *The Way He Looks* (2014) and *The Snowman* (2017).

Unfortunately, the judicial system still asks many of the same mother-blaming questions associated with outdated science, though perhaps they aren't as obvious today as they were in the 1950s. From pickpockets to serial killers and terrorists, the starting point for *why* is usually the criminal's family of origin, which loosely translates to Freud's first question: "So, can you tell me about your mother?" Mother-blaming is a dangerous oversimplification of a person's identity and choices, as it can be used to excuse a child's behavior and unfairly place blame on the shoulders of the one who bore them. To reiterate, parents certainly have great influence on the development of their child's overall personhood, but in the absence of abuse/neglect dynamics, nothing is fair about using the position of *mother* as a scapegoat. In Susan's case, she was victim-blamed *and* mother-blamed.

Domestic Violence

Tim's defense made sure Susan was blamed for her own murder straightaway, and the subconsciously rampant mother-blaming assumption was helpful to their defense, but the second account on which Susan was victim-blamed was with regard to the domestic violence present in the Roman home.

The defensive wounds found on Susan's body, unrelated to her cause of death, suggested a pattern of physical violence that she most certainly did not inflict upon herself. Those closest to the Romans knew of Tim's poor emotional regulation skills, evidenced in his angry outbursts, general agitation, and the freedom he felt to visit his emotions on his mother. His temperamental behavior could have been related to the steroid and testosterone dosing he regularly received and related hormonal imbalance noted at trial, but regardless of the *why*, he had long been understood as a short-fused, volatile guy by his family, peers, clinicians, and instructors.

Dr. Carl Faber's testimony added particularly damning brushstrokes onto Susan's portrait in court. He said he empathized deeply with Tim and believed Susan "brought those fears to Tim for hundreds of hours." He claimed Susan "could not hold on to reality…it would be like she had an IQ of 60." He also testified that he found her terribly "draining" on him during sessions and that Tim was "provoked by aggressive, irrational behavior by his mother."

Dr. Paula J. Caplan in the anthology *Bad Mothers: The Politics of Blame in the Twentieth-Century America* says:

> *A psychotherapy patient reveals her most intimate feelings and her most shameful secrets to her therapist. Her therapist learns things about her that no one else has ever known. She goes to the therapist seeking help both to feel better and to learn more of the truth about herself and her life. This gives the therapist enormous power over her. Because the training for most therapists involves so much mother-blame and woman-blame, only the unusual ones help the patient go beyond mother-blame and self-blame. Traditional therapists tend to believe sincerely that mother-blaming fits reality, and they regard themselves as helping their patients to accept this reality. Thus, women are primed to accept the therapist's descriptions of them and their mothers—or themselves as mother—as manipulative, overprotective, intrusive, cold, rejecting, and so on.*

Faber's testimony was just what the defense needed to complete the painting.

Media Circus

"Hollywood" and "murder" are two topics that *always* sell, and when put together, they usually have twice the selling power. Whether Susan was an A-lister or not was of little interest to the media after her death, because any Hollywood connection interests the masses. Papers capitalized on her Hollywood career to sell the story of her murder, which may have been a prudent business strategy, but it did nothing but confuse the general public on who Susan Cabot Roman really was and what type of crime had really been committed by her son, Timothy Scott Roman. Media distortions are common, and often unintentional, but with mass dissemination of mass content, there are bound to be blunders.

One of the most confounding aspects of the news reports of the case was how reporters and readers alike drew on the on-screen information available about Susan. They perhaps unconsciously identified similarities between fact and fiction and allowed a mix of both to fill in the gaps. The diabolical fact-fiction cocktail the masses were consuming in the 1980s about Susan Cabot Roman fostered not only untruths, but the extent of victim-blaming present in the case.

Fans have forever confused on-screen details with off-screen ones; it just comes with more consequences in the context of murder. One of the greatest radio examples of this fact-fiction blurring (besides the obvious *War of the Worlds* one) was shared by actor Jean Hersholt. In CBS's long-running radio series *Dr. Christian*, Hersholt played the kindly, small-town doctor who encountered ailments and dramas of all kinds in his practice. Fans of the show apparently found Hersholt so convincing as the good doctor that he regularly received fan mail soliciting medical advice throughout the run of the show.

"Confirmation bias is the human tendency to search for, favor, and use information that confirms one's pre-existing views on a certain topic," says Harvard Business School staff writer Patrick Healy (2016). And confirmation bias was what fueled the overarching spirit of victim-blaming in Susan's case—both in and out of court. Lucky for the defense, the masses had already been primed for fictionalized accounts of the life and death of Susan Cabot Roman.

The connections media and the masses made between Susan's life and Janice Starlin's in Roger Corman's *Wasp Woman* were obvious, and the similarities can seem a little eerie if framed the right way. The element of the "experimental injections" was oddly categorized in both fact and fiction in Susan's case, but ultimately, that's where the similarities between Susan's life and the film begin and end.

The storyline of *Wasp Woman* and Susan's antagonistic character portrayal in *Sorority Girl* fostered perceived "confirmation" of Tim's "she had it coming" defense. Similarly, the storylines and character names in *The*

Prince Who Was a Thief and *Son of Ali Baba* fostered perceived "confirmation" that Tim was of royal Middle-Eastern blood. The ancillary issue of Tim's father's identity was naturally a source of fascination.

The themes of both foreign adventure films relate to mistaken identity, and some of the character names in both films are coincidentally the same as King Hussein of Jordan's. These coincidences, of course, don't mean a thing, but try explaining that to public opinion in the midst of a voltaic murder trial.

This fact-fiction blurring greatly swayed public opinion on the case. Certainly, public opinion is not what Tim's sentencing hinged on, but public opinion is always significant in how any public figure's legacy is preserved.

During the press fury, no one seemed to recall the charitable notices from Susan's career, for they were too busy using confirmation bias to their advantage. Philanthropy doesn't sell. Carnage does. No one cared that for years, Susan had visited terminally ill children in hospitals all over the country on her publicity tours, donated thousands to buy Christmas gifts for underprivileged children in the United States and the United Kingdom, and had never in her life turned a benefit performance down. No one cared that she had friends and family who loved her deeply and vehemently denied the litany of accusations the defense came up with. No one cared about Susan's desperate years of frantic lobbying for Tim's medical treatment. No one cared about the single mother's plight of raising a medically and behaviorally complex child with little to no lifelines.

No one cared because those details went against the overarching narrative. Would the story of Susan's death have been as compelling if everyone had left her in the role of the victim? Would as many newspapers have sold if Tim had been declared the monster and she the physical and psychological hostage? I don't know, but it was easier to draw on the fiction of her filmography than the fact of her humanity.

***

Neighbors who were interviewed by the papers described the Romans as a quiet household with little obvious activity inside or out. One neighbor said Tim seemed "very dependent on Susan," who was "pleasant, but *different*." There were rumors mother and son were so inseparable that they were actually lovers, but of course that was all hype with no substantiation. Many believed Susan herself manifested her own slaying through her abuse of Tim; she was never seen as a victim, only a villainess of mad-scientist persuasion, with Tim as her prime experiment, you know, in *Wasp Woman* fashion.

All of Tim's attorneys and those who testified on his behalf, including Michael Roman and Dr. Faber, emphasized narrow perspectives of Susan's last few years and painted an elaborate picture of her as a mentally ill viper with poor little Tim as her prey. Whether it was true or not didn't matter to the defense, because it worked. Tim pled not guilty by reason of insanity to the initial first-degree murder charge.

Though Tim was the one technically on trial, Susan was really the one tried and convicted. Tim was painted as a lifelong victim of a vain, venomous mother who had come completely unhinged and he, having no other choice, beat her to death. Dr. Faber even went so far as to insinuate on the stand that Susan would probably have committed suicide anyway if Tim had not snapped and essentially put her out of her misery. "I don't have a timeframe in my mind for what happened. All I remember is seeing my mom on the bed and apparently, she was dead," Tim said.

Tim often had blackouts and suffered from memory loss that made it difficult to obtain veracious testimony. One of Tim's therapists, Dr. John Watkins, testified that Tim had severe memory lapses that affected his ability to recall significant amounts of his past. It wasn't black and white with Tim because he was capable in many areas, but utterly inadequate in other basic ones, and there didn't seem to be a recognized pattern to his strengths and weaknesses. Though he had a litany of medical conditions, he had no definite mental diagnosis that could explain or categorize his level of functionality, motives, or judgment. The lack of categorization was in the defense's favor, because Susan did suffer from PTSD, depression, and anxiety, and those diagnoses were easier to implicate in the indirect "cause" of Tim's behavior, even if environmentally.

Susan and Tim had complicated relational dynamics and had many advisors in both of their lives who didn't provide the help and accountability perhaps they should have. Many of those advisors were all too willing to throw Susan and Tim both under the bus during the trial. Incidentally, none of their "advisors," including Chester Leo Smith and Dr. Carl Faber, apparently saw enough lunacy in the dynamics between Susan and Tim when mother and son were using their services regularly to intervene. Smith visited the Romans' Charmion Lane home regularly before Susan's murder and apparently found neither her nor their home deplorable enough to either report her or, at the very least, decline subsequent invitations. During proceedings, he claimed the two had lived in "filth and chaos" for years and years.

Similarly, Dr. Carl Faber made a great witness for the defense, as he was more than willing to join the painting strokes of "Norma Desmond," though he did nothing to advocate for the woman who entrusted her intimate life details to him for over thirty years. Dr. Faber was cross-examined by Deputy District Attorney Bradford E. Stone, and one of the most poignant points he brought up was Faber's position as a mandated reporter.

In 1974, Congress passed the Child Abuse Prevention and Treatment Act (CAPTA) Public Law 93-247 that helped fund the establishment of Child Protective Services (CPS) to prevent incidents of child abuse in the United States. In accordance with the CAPTA, professional individuals such as teachers, clergy, or mental health providers were considered mandated reporters of child abuse. Mandated reporters were charged with the ethical and professional responsibility to notify CPS and/or police with any suspicions of abuse, no matter how unspecified. The CAPTA is certainly still in effect today, and failure to report is considered a felony in some states.

Definitionally, the four primary categories of "child abuse" are: physical abuse, emotional abuse, sexual abuse, and neglect. According to the defense's portrait of Susan, her parenting style at least hit two of those categories on the head. Stone's main inquiry of Faber was: If he knew the alleged deplorable condition of the Romans' home and the allegedly deplorable parenting practices of Susan Cabot Roman, why in the devil didn't he report it to the proper authorities? He tried to answer the question using poetry to no avail. Ultimately, he backtracked on his knowledge of the home's condition and Susan's treatment of Tim to save his own neck.

All of the double-crossing on the stand wasn't a conspiracy against Susan, of course, but it was the easier route for Tim. And in the non-juried second trial, Judge Schempp bought it lock, stock, and barrel.

In the stacks and stacks of Tim's medical records that were examined during proceedings, there were more than a few clues of Tim's lifelong struggles. One of his pediatricians wrote of then eleven-year-old Tim: "an emotionally immature, somewhat disturbed child who is having difficulty handling the demands of growing up." One of his psychologists in 1971 implicated Susan's "overmothering" in Tim's behavior: "Much of the youngster's immature behavior has been inappropriately reinforced by his mother…being an actress, tends to be somewhat overly dramatic and overly concerned." In Susan's defense, the question became: does overmothering always or even usually result in matricide? A healthy dose of resentment perhaps, but murder?

Throughout the trial, Tim accused Susan of all sorts of bizarre things, like forcing him to play with a Ouija board, locking him outside, and making him sleep in a shed if his chores weren't completed in time, but none of those accusations were ever substantiated. Whether true or not, the accounts only furthered the narrative that Susan was a psychotic monster who enjoyed torturing her only child. Of course, there is much more evidence to support the contrary, however. Tom Weaver said, "Never once did I hear Susan raise her voice to Tim or show any anger at the fact that he would diss her. Never did anything but act like Tim was the center of her life."

Tim's second, non-jury trial in 1989 lasted six days. Despite the evidence investigators found of premeditation, Van Nuys Superior Court Judge Darlene E. Schempp ultimately found Tim not guilty of murder in the first degree. "There is no question that the defendant loved his mother very much," the Judge said. In 1989, Tim was ultimately charged with involuntary manslaughter because Judge Darlene Schempp said Tim convinced her through proceedings that his act of killing was "not the result of a criminal mind." He was sentenced to three years' probation during which he was required to obtain psychological counseling and pay a $1,000 fine.

Evidence Ignored

The portrait of Susan as the perpetrator overrode the portrait of Tim as one. The evidence of Susan's myriad defensive wounds, though unrelated to her cause of death, was never adequately considered in the overall picture of the mother-son relationship Susan and Tim had.

Because Susan was found in only a purple V-neck negligée, and because of some vague mention in police reports about Tim's briefs being found near her body, a sexual assault kit was ordered, but no specific findings were noted that suggested Susan was assaulted before or after her death. The strange sexual current of the case, however, was something that lingered even through Tim's trial, partially because of Susan's attire and status as a silver screen beauty, and partially because of Tim's odd behavior and statements.

Deputy Masuda noted his observations at the crime scene:

The decedent was dressed only in a nightgown, a bra was found at the foot of the bed. Due to the statements regarding sexual matters by Timothy Roman, and the condition in which the decedent was found, Criminalist Manhay was requested to respond.

Manhay collected samples through the sexual assault kit that had been requested. The "sexual matters" Tim reportedly talked about were vaguely described in police reports: "Reportedly, the son, Timothy Roman, told police that he and his mother were very close, and that they would talk about anything, including intimate sexual matters." No one ever seemed to get clarity on those particular comments of Tim's, but then again, Tim said and did all kinds of things no one could ever interpret. Whether or not Susan was ever sexually assaulted by Tim remains unknown, but the evidence of so many defensive wounds from previous encounters, nearly all over her entire body, clearly demonstrates she was physically injured by him outside the context of her death.

Several of Tim's and Susan's doctors testified on her behalf, but the narrative had already been decided long before the verdict. The narrative of Susan as a maniacal "Norma Desmond" was easier for the majority to go with somehow, leaving jury members and Judge Schempp to casually graze over any testimony or evidence that contradicted that portrait.

The violence that Tim had so obviously perpetrated against Susan over the span of at least the last few years of her life was also ignored by the court. Though the defensive wounds were in fact brought up by the prosecution, the defense was quick to come in with misogynistic red herrings of "she started it," or "if only she hadn't been so overbearing," or "if only she hadn't been a hoarder." The defense preferred to talk about Susan's lack of housekeeping and whether she'd had men spend the night since her divorce from Michael Roman instead of the fact that her brains were beaten out while she slept. In tandem with the rape culture rhetoric, if Susan were a poor housekeeper and had co-ed sleepovers, clearly, she was making herself a target for murder. Chester Leo Smith's victim-blaming, mother-blaming statements were possibly the worst of all heard in the case. His comment about Susan "suffer[ing] recurrent mental breakdowns and drew into a reclusive existence into her home...hidden from the outside world [which] exacerbated her son's emotional and developmental retardation" is one of the most obvious examples of victim-blaming and mother-blaming I've ever read. In absurdity, it ranks right up there with Leo Kanner's refrigerator mother theory to explain autism.

If not for the spin framing, the evidence by itself was plenty to convict Timothy Scott Roman of child-to-parent violence that eventually led to matricide, but such evidence was framed and hung next to the portrait of Susan Cabot Roman, movie star, painted by a fleet of misogynistic victim-blaming, mother-blaming "experts."

Matricide

According to B. O'Connell's early 1960s study of matricide, it was found that "a son who kills his mother is usually an unmarried, unambitious young man with an intense relationship with his mother, a feeling of social inferiority, and an absent or passive father." Categorically, Tim Roman meets every criterion purported by O'Connell and other experts in the psychological analysis of men who kill their mothers. Between 1977 and the year in which Susan was murdered, more than three hundred parents were killed each year by their own children.

In West and Feldsher's 2010 study, they found sons who commit matricide are "often immature, passive, and dependent; schizophrenia is common; single and living with mother; fathers absent." West and Feldsher also describe the victims of matricide as "often domineering, demanding, and possessive; often the only victim."

In a study conducted by Dominique Bourget, Pierre Gagné, and Mary-Eve Labelle in 2007, the parallels found between Timothy Roman and other males found guilty of matricide are startling. In the majority of cases, Bourget, Gagné, and Labelle found perpetrators were, like Tim, residing in the same home with their mothers at the time of the killing. They also found that the most common weapon used to commit matricide was, like in Tim's case, a blunt instrument. Most killings, like Susan's, largely occurred without warning.

Though there are scholarly categorizations we can theoretically place around such acts of violence, there are few true defenses for such. Mother-killers are generally placed in specific criminal profiles that often contain psychotic features. As heinous a crime as matricide, it, like most things, goes back to the beginning of time. Some of the most widely referenced cases range from Cleopatra III of Egypt, who was assassinated in 101 BC by order of her son, to the Sandy Hook gunman, Adam Lanza, who shot and killed his mother before killing twenty elementary school children and six of the school's staff members in 2012.

Many correlative explanations have been offered for the root of murderous motivations in the cases of sons who are suddenly overcome with brutal intent for the one who bore them. Among them are echoes of what Tim's attorneys suggested about his relationship with Susan: the old "she made him do it" routine. The major problem with that argument in Tim's case, however, is whenever that defense logically failed, they systematically relied upon a plethora of excuses from his developmental challenges, the human growth hormone experiment, steroids, the devil, etc.

In Kathleen Heide and Autumn Frie's 2010 critique of the literature on matricide, they report:

Russell (1984) emphasized how dysfunctional parental relationships, internalized threatening circumstances, and intense conflict and provocation can lead to matricide. He argued that the response to these acts should focus on a therapeutic approach as opposed to a punitive one.

Judge Schempp passed down Tim's final judgment from a perspective similar to Russell's "therapeutic approach," though it's unclear what "more therapy" truly did for Tim during his probation. Did he go on to kill again? No, but a sentence of more therapy also did little to vindicate Susan or discourage the violence involved. Tim wasn't perceived as a threat to the public at large, but with his varied history of psychotic episodes, regular outpatient therapy was considered synonymous with an acquittal by some. Schempp said, "Roman and his mother both had physical and emotional problems that may have contributed to the slaying," again, charging Susan with her own murder.

Tim's trial was among Judge Darlene Schempp's first as a criminal court judge. She had a long career on the bench after Tim's sentencing, but she was notorious for celebrity cases, controversial decisions, and passing down unusually light sentencing. The district attorney called her "no-prison sentence" record "an invitation to commit murder."

In a 2000 criminal case, Schempp reportedly gave the defendant who was charged with assaulting someone with an AK-47 a lighter sentence because she learned he had experienced abuse as a child.

Schempp handed down a sentence similar to Tim's in the 2001 capital murder case against actor Robert Blake, who was accused of killing his wife, Bonny Lee Bakley. Though Blake was found liable for her wrongful death by another court in 2005, Schempp was quoted by *The Los Angeles Times* as saying, "I think the evidence there is so speculative that it carries very little weight" before letting the accused "walk out of the Van Nuys courtroom a free man." Schempp took great pity on Timothy Scott Roman and invited the "Norma Desmond" portrait of Susan into court proceedings, which ultimately influenced Tim's sentencing. Tim bludgeoning Susan's brains out while she slept wasn't an "act of a criminal mind" according to Schempp, yet in another case, she called a gypsy fortune teller's money racket "cruel and vicious."

Tim's defense attorney, Michael White, said after sentencing was passed down:

This case is a real tragic one. It's hard to walk out and say you're happy with the result. He loved his mother and…is relieved in the knowledge he doesn't have to go to jail and can get on and live his life.

The prosecution's statement post-verdict wasn't a whole lot better: "I'm not dissatisfied with the verdict," Deputy District Attorney Bradford Stone said, "Based on evidence presented by the defense, it became real obvious that he did not premeditate the slaying. I still get the gut feeling that he just snapped from the stress of living with his mother all those years."

Tom Weaver spent quite a bit of time with both Susan and Tim in the mid-1980s until her death. Regarding the verdict, Tom said in a 2000 *E!* interview:

It just seemed like the victim becoming the accused. After she died, I was reading the paper what a 'nut' she supposedly was, I tried very hard to remember incidents where she was irrational or said crazy things and honestly, I couldn't think of anything other than doting on Timothy too much.

Despite the testimony used to paint Susan as a real-life "Wasp Woman" in her volatility, actress Kathleen Hughes, who was a close friend of hers for decades, in a 2000 *E!* interview, said to those accusations: "I never saw any signs of Susan being mentally unbalanced firsthand.

She was a lovely person. She was a good friend. She was a little neurotic, but everybody is."

Michael

Michael Roman supported Tim at every turn of his trials, but weary of the media circus, Michael left California not long after Tim was sentenced to his probationary period. Michael moved to Virginia, where he remarried and became a successful financial advisor for decades. He died on May 17 of 2023 at the age of eighty. In his obituary, Timothy Scott Roman was listed as his only child.

Muriel

Muriel was present at Susan's funeral and throughout court proceedings for both of Tim's trials. She petitioned the court to visit Tim while he was incarcerated, and she was granted visits with him. As heartbreaking as it assuredly was for her on all sides, she supported her only grandchild until the end. She died on November 21, 1998, at the age of ninety-seven.

Tim's Real Father

Susan went to her grave without divulging the identity of Tim's biological father. It is possible that Tim himself may not have even known from whom he received half of his DNA. During proceedings, the question of course arose. In April of 1989, Tim's first defense attorney, Chester Leo Smith, attempted to have him transported out of the general public Los Angeles County Hall of Justice to solitary confinement in Van Nuys because he was experiencing much of the same victimization by other inmates that he had experienced in school. The warden wasn't as compassionate as Susan had been in walking him to and from his classes to avoid his bullies, so in petitioning the court for his move to another jail, they said as the alleged son of King Hussein of Jordan, Tim was facing all kinds of harassment over his "half-Jewish half-Arab descent," though his lineage had never been confirmed despite accounts of DNA testing during the trials. "The Sheriff is directed to hold the defendant Timothy Scott Roman separate and apart from the other inmates, while in lockup of the Van Nuys Courthouse," court records noted.

There was also a report that circulated claiming monthly deposits into Susan's bank account were traced to a trust fund in Jordan. The papers explained the "stipend" as obvious child support, though Michael Roman vehemently denied the accuracy of those reports.

The reports of monthly deposits caused both the defense and the prosecution to lobby for DNA testing to at long last reveal the identity of Tim's biological father. Judge Schempp denied the requests. Schempp said it was irrelevant to the case and would only amplify the media circus and potentially bring other parties into what were already tense and terrible proceedings. Tim himself didn't seem particularly interested in finding out who his biological father was. Court records show that actor Chris Jones petitioned the court to visit Tim while he was incarcerated, awaiting his second trial. Tim's first attorney, Chester Leo Smith, later told Michael Roman: "Mike, this guy Christopher Jones came to see Tim, and if ever a father and son looked alike, they did in this instance." Aside from Smith's very non-scientific assertion that Chris and Tim looked alike, there was no evidence to suggest Chris was Tim's father, only speculation.

In short, Tim's father could be any of the handsome suitors Susan was dating just before she learned of her pregnancy in mid-1963. For someone supposedly so fraught with neuroticism, she sure kept it classy in never kissing and telling or complicating the situation for Tim's biological father, whoever he is or was.

Tim

Who knows what Timothy Scott Roman's sentencing "should" have been if anything different than it was. Timothy was assuredly a victim of science more than a victim of his mother. The main issue with the outcome of Tim's trials is not so much in his sentencing as in the erroneous narrative constructed around the true crime victim. In giving Tim every benefit of the doubt, perhaps he wasn't cognitively capable of understanding the implications of acting on such murderous impulses, but he was apparently capable of premeditation and hiding evidence.

The Superior Court of the State of California for the County of Los Angeles issued the following in the initial case summary:

> *On or about December 10, 1986, in the County of Los Angeles, the crime of MURDER, in violation of PENAL CODE SECTION 187(a), a Felony, was committed by TIMOTHY SCOTT ROMAN, who did willfully, unlawfully, and with malice aforethought murder Susan Cabot Roman, a human being.*

Somewhere along the way, the whole "Susan Cabot Roman, *human being*" piece got lost in the newspaper frenzy. Despite the verdict of involuntary manslaughter and his light sentence of three years' probation, Tim intentionally went into Susan's room while she slept and intentionally beat her to death. Was there chemical interference in his body and brain at the time? Yes. Did he still murder his mom while she slept? Also, yes.

During Tim's incarceration awaiting trial, in January 1988, he joined the thousands of others in filing a lawsuit against the medical groups that issued the experimental treatments for "human growth hormone." More than 25,000 children worldwide who had diagnoses similar to Tim's were given these injections from 1958 to 1985. Unbeknownst to anyone at the time, the enzymes taken from cadavers were contaminated, despite a purification process, with fatal Creutzfeldt-Jakob Disease (CJD) properties. In the early 1980s, after the first few CJD deaths in the United States that were correlated with the human growth hormone study, a synthetic version was used in place of the organic cadaver enzymes, but studies continued.

By the late 1980s, hundreds of lawsuits had been filed globally against governmental entities that funded the experimental studies. Many sued on the grounds of "psychiatric injury," as participants were told they may have been exposed to CJD, for which there is no cure. Just the knowledge that one might suddenly exhibit symptoms of the fatal condition nearly at any moment would be enough for anyone to experience tremendous psychological duress.

In Tim's case, his defense team thought filing would help finger the study for his murderous impulses, but CJD doesn't really work quite like that. In the case of the 25,000 study participants, the CJD agent remained dormant in their systems, in some cases for decades, but when it activated, the debilitation was rapid, and death was often within a few weeks from onset. In other words, out of the 25,000 study participants, Tim was the only one who committed matricide.

In 1988, *The Los Angeles Times* reported:

But Roman is afraid he may be infected with the disease, and his attorney has argued that the CJD agent, which causes dementia, could have played a role in Cabot's murder by so severely clouding the brain of her son. But doctors say that, if Roman was displaying symptoms of the disease when his mother was killed in 1986, he would probably be critically ill or dead today.

After sentencing, twenty-five-year-old Tim was released into the care of Michael Roman's mother, Elizabeth Roman. He spent two and a half years behind bars in between trials in the Los Angeles County Hall of Justice and completed his probation in his adoptive grandmother Elizabeth's care. The two reportedly got on swimmingly together for the first few years after Tim's sentencing. Michael Roman said in a 2000 *E!* interview:

My mom and Tim were together from let's say '88, '89, when we moved out of the house, 'til the day he died in 2003. And they were like two kids. My mom had a miserable life. We come from Europe, and she had just a tumultuous life. So the two of 'em hit it off. They were living their lives together as two kids. They were both taking art classes and going on trips, everywhere together. They really liked each other. And my mom was very protective.

In Tim's last years, Elizabeth and Tim became a vibrant version of "Susan and Tim."

Much of Tim's maladaptive behavior reportedly grew worse, however, as he aged until it was undeniable that the CJD had emerged from its incubated state in Tim's body from the contaminated "experimental injections." Though he had been administered the injections twenty years before, the enzymes extracted from cadavers activated in his body after two decades of dormancy. As the disease began to come alive, Tim slipped further and further from reality until he was placed in a nursing facility close to Elizabeth's home in Azusa. He eventually went from bizarre behavior to unconsciousness, and he died at age thirty-nine on January 22, 2003.

Three years before he died, he made his last public statement about his mother in a 2000 *E!* interview:

My mom's life story is important... and not to judge me and certainly not to judge her. I think that she was a great, creative person. She had a lot to offer. She was very much interested in art, in painting.

She was herself a fantastic paintress. I would say her paintings are very good. Whatever that sadness was, whatever the problems were, it interfered in her becoming what she could have been. This illness had such a grip on her, or she allowed it to possess her. I think if she had had a normal family life, that I'm sure she would probably be on the top.... Probably the best things I remember about her is that she was a very sweet person.

Susan — "Person of Valor"

Like everyone, Susan Cabot Roman had her humanity, but probably more emotional scars than the average person, considering her tumultuous childhood and difficulties in adulthood as a single mom to a child with unusual challenges. Was she a bit neurotic like Kathleen Hughes suggested? Probably. Was she a viperous "Norma Desmond" who lived to torture her only child? No. Did she deserve to die by the hands of her child that she loved more than life itself? Definitely not.

She reportedly only learned of the fatal potential side effects of the injections in 1985, when the first case of Creutzfeldt-Jakob Disease was found in a participant of the experimental human growth hormone study. It was breaking news in the papers, and devastating to parents like Susan who had so trustingly tried to do what was best for their children. Though CJD had certainly been discovered years before in other contexts, the discovery of its presence in the human growth hormone study was shocking. That meant the contamination containing the CJD agent could have affected the entire population of study participants: 25,000 children worldwide. After discussing the news article with Tim's physicians, Susan was almost incapacitated with self-blame. The contamination could have meant anything from Tim's past and present difficulties to a wretched, early death from the disease that could "activate" at "any second." *The Los Angeles Times* reported in 1988: "There is no cure for the disease and no way to diagnose it until symptoms appear. But that can be up to thirty years from the time it is contracted, so hormone recipients and their parents must simply wait." That looming fear alone is enough to drive anyone to a bedridden state of depression and anxiety.

Susan Cabot Roman was much more than the painting hung by the papers and court proceedings after her death. She was an intelligent, intricate, resourceful woman who took a prisoned childhood full of trauma, and independently made something beautiful emerge from it.

The fame and fortune are always remarkable feats for anyone, but given the agony of her upbringing, what is even more remarkable is her tenacity to overcome many of the residuals of such. She loved Timothy Scott Roman with every fiber of her being, and that was probably her greatest fault. Was she perfect? No. Was she always level-headed and completely mature in her engagements with Tim? No. Could she be emotionally reactive and unreasonable? Absolutely. But I do not believe her motivation for perhaps over-mothering at times was ever grounded in anything but love for Tim, and I believe after careful study of her life, given her context, she did the absolute best she could for her son.

Unfortunately, even her "best" wasn't well-suited to the complicated outcomes in Tim's case, but if she had been able to see the future and somehow knew what lay ahead, I suspect she wouldn't have loved Tim any less. As a matter of fact, from whatever ethereal plane she may have observed proceedings in the afterlife, she may have welcomed the desecration of her entire legacy in order for courts to pass down Tim a lighter sentence.

Harriet Pearl Shapiro, or Susan Cabot Roman, was given a beautiful private service by Malinow Silverman Mortuary in Westwood, California on January 9, 1987. In her eulogy, LAPD Westside reserve chaplain Rabbi Henry Kraus said of her to the intimate crowd of family and friends: "Susan was a person of valor, a devoted mother and daughter throughout her life…We can hardly find expression for our feeling. She loved her mother, her only child, and her friends. Her death is a mystery of which we can say nothing. Faith is the only thing that gives us consolation." Faith for Susan fell somewhere between the paradox of reformed Judaism and Christianity. Both religions hold fast to the passage in Ecclesiastes of life after earthly death:

> *Remember him—before the silver cord is severed, and the golden bowl is broken; before the pitcher is shattered at the spring, and the wheel broken at the well, and the dust returns to the ground it came from, and the spirit returns to God who gave it.*

Susan was buried in an unmarked grave at Culver City's Hillside Memorial Park. In 2012, she was given a marker by petition.

***

As Susan herself once said in an interview describing the many twists and turns of her career: "All this happened because I didn't have fare to Italy."

Chapter Nine
Final Discussion and Call to Action

"Injustice anywhere is a threat to justice everywhere. We are caught in an inescapable network of mutuality, tied in a single garment of destiny. Whatever affects one directly, affects all indirectly."

— Martin Luther King Jr.

Thirty-seven years after the death of B-movie queen Susan Cabot, her full-length biography is finally written. Why? One of the things that makes stories like Susan's so captivating despite the years that have passed is the impossibility of true closure. The story is as old as time itself: a situation seems fine on the surface, disaster strikes, and we're all left with unanswered questions and awful emotions incited by "what ifs" and "could have beens." I believe one of the primary reasons the legend of the *Titanic* is still such an addictive topic in our culture more than one hundred years later is because of this very principle. Our humanity craves closure on the flip side of catastrophe, and when we simply can't have it, we spin on the information available to us, however incomplete it may be. I think one of the many things prohibiting closure in Susan's case is the injustice in it all—injustice that led to her death and injustice of her murderer's sentencing.

Much like the *Titanic*, Susan was a shining icon of glamor and fortitude, until disaster struck in the dead of night. In collecting pieces of the puzzle left strewn about in various sources, I have not attempted to solve anything, but rather place the fragments of her triumphs and challenges into a new mosaic called: redemption.

This book was written in part to memorialize the fascinating life and career of a woman whose legacy, in my opinion, was victimized by the media and her son's defense team. Susan's is a clear case of victim-blaming that not only let Tim's responsibility off the hook, but nationally fostered the principles of rape culture and male privilege. In part because of how Susan's death was publicly framed, it was easier for the masses to say, "Oh, so she was a terrible mother, and her son killed her. Got it. So, what's the latest update on those tax increases?" As electric as the story was, its framing placed her murder among the trivial.

It should be noted that as Susan's biographer, I had serious reservations about including such lengthy, graphic portions of her autopsy report in this book; however, I ultimately decided it was necessary to explicitly show what bizarre and severe acts of violence Tim perpetrated on his mother. The inclusion of these graphic details is in no way intended as an exploitation of Susan herself, but because of the whitewashed portrait of Timothy Scott Roman in the media, I felt it was important to share the raw, documented information on *exactly* how Tim killed his mother. While I merely shared some of the most pertinent portions of Susan's autopsy that the coroner provided in court, Tim's ultimate involuntary manslaughter charge and sentencing in relation to that extent of violence is hard to comprehend. In weighing Tim's charge and sentencing against the disturbing particulars of Susan's physical death, this alone is plenty to confirm the presence of "victim-blaming" in this case.

Julia Churchill Schoellkopf (2012) says, "It is easier to blame the victim because it psychologically solves the problem for individuals and society: as long as you are good and do not behave a certain way, you will not be raped" (or killed). In Susan's case, it was easier for the public to see her death as some "spooky" real-life manifestation of her film career in sci-fi than to identify with her as a victim of murder.

One of my primary motivations to write this comprehensive account of Susan was to systematically draw out the universal truths that lie between the lines of Susan Cabot Roman's story. If we can't have a satisfying sense of closure at the end of a story (which stories of brutal murder never seem to give that to us), sometimes we fit the details into the framework of a cautionary tale. I argue that Susan's story holds many universal truths relevant to her era and ours in the 2020s.

Ownership, Bad Counsel, & A Bunch of Bystanders

Because trauma attached itself to Susan's story so early in her life and really never seemed to leave, she never truly had a lasting sense of ownership over her own life's trajectory. From Boston as a child to Los Angeles as a young adult, Susan was "owned" by someone or some entity for nearly the entire course of her life. The state of Massachusetts "owned" her after her father abandoned their family, and her mother was committed. The infamous old Hollywood studio system "owned" her for years beyond just the course of her contract with Universal-International, as it did so many thousands of starlets on both the A and B lists. Studios and the media considered actors and actresses of the Golden Era to be their eternal possessions. This may seem like an exaggeration, but the greatest proof of this assertion is the media circus surrounding Susan's death and Tim's trial. In other words, no matter how "small" her roles may have been under contract, she was forever known to the public as "a movie star." This categorization no doubt comes with blessings and curses, but perhaps more of the latter when it comes to murder. Her eternal position as a celebrity is evidenced in the countless newspaper reports that used her Hollywood career to sell the story of her death. Would there have been such a capitalizing opportunity if she had not been a silver screen starlet once upon a time?

In her last years, she was again "owned" by the inescapable dynamic she helped create between her and Tim. There's little doubt that Susan felt increasingly cornered in her own home as Tim grew older and his psychotic tendencies grew more potent. Though to a certain degree she admitted to herself and those closest to her that Tim's behavior was completely out of control by the time he reached his teenage years, my personal belief is that she lived in fear of him. The extent of Tim's volatility frightened her, and the extent of her own love for him also frightened her. I have reason to believe she carefully considered the options for Tim and his future, and while she could have chosen to place him in a facility, her love for him *and* her need for him would not allow her to do that. It was easier for her to spiral with him than to try to be the voice of accountability when she herself had so much unresolved woundedness. Susan lived in a pressure cooker with Tim, and when walking through the kitchen feels the same as walking through a minefield because you never know what version of someone you'll be met with, your own home isn't even home anymore. That type of looming volatility is enough to drive anyone mad.

Susan was, on one hand, owned by the three systems mentioned above, but she was also terribly dependent upon others such as her husbands and lovers, psychologists such as Dr. Carl Faber, and Tim himself. Feeling so out of control within one's own story certainly feeds into a sense of overdependence on the scant few beacons of stability she encountered in her life.

As a former psychotherapist myself, I believe many of the psychologists Susan and Tim went to regularly for years did both of them a great disservice from beginning to end. It was a different era with different modalities and different ideologies on the disciplines of human psychology, but from my postmodern point of view this side of the 1980s, in short, what the hell were these experts thinking?

For someone like Susan who grew up in an era that espoused the rigid "just shut up and deal with your traumas quietly please," it was a great testament to her character that she sought mental health assistance to begin with. To go against the majority and stigma and initiate one's own healing process is more than a feat! It's obvious she longed for healing and instead of turning to maladaptive coping mechanisms that would have perhaps given her an early rap sheet, she went to therapy for answers. For anyone who finds the courage to do such a thing as initiate their own journey of healing, I find that heroic.

The great dance of dependence, however, with Dr. Faber and others like him who counseled Susan (and later Tim) for years, I have to resort to a headshake because Susan was a fragile, naïve person who, with the right type of empowerment therapy, could have met her objectives in healing rather than rowing further away from them. These psychologists she saw were, in fact, professionals, so I do not discredit their authenticity, but I do have to question where their boundaries, ethics, and commitment to "first do no harm" were in their treatment of Susan and Tim.

If Dr. Faber truly saw such suicidal despair in Susan upon their last meeting as he testified, why was there no safety intervention? Therapists today get sued and stripped of their licenses for far less. He was a mandated reporter by law for his clients' immediate safety, and in my opinion, he dropped the ball to the detriment of all three members of the Roman family. If the dynamics (particularly between mother and son) were so obviously acidic that "everyone knew about it," why was Faber's prescription simply "more counseling sessions?"

Susan wasn't the only client of Faber's to meet an untimely and potentially preventable end. William "Bill" Everett Kane was another longtime client and personal friend of Faber's. When he committed suicide in October of 1991, authorities found his death was premeditated down to the most minute detail. He wanted a Dixieland band at his funeral and Dr. Carl Faber to give his eulogy. It is unknown if Faber knew of Kane's plans to commit suicide, but his statement was curiously detached when questioned about Kane's legacy: "A lot of how you felt about Bill depended on whether you believed him or not. If you believed him, you had to take his life at face value and you could see why he did what he did."

Unfortunately, Faber had another close associate of his die by their own hand: his wife. On April 12, 1992, Faber's wife, Dr. Gail Stevenson, who was a clinical psychologist and devout feminist, shot herself in the head in her West LA private practice. Just six months before her death, Stevenson had opened a feminist bookstore called Revolution that had "developed into a significant gathering place and community resource for Westside feminists, artists, and political progressives." Stevenson explained to *The Los Angeles Times* her passion behind opening the bookstore:

> *A lot of women in psychotherapy cannot find the words to express their anger and feelings and they often get sick because of it. What I am trying*

to do is provide a place with materials from a woman's perspective that really reflect what women think, feel, and say and that you wouldn't find anywhere else.

When Stevenson's body was found, Faber gave the statement that his wife had no history of clinical depression, but he believed her suicidal ideation was brought about by her "personal pain and despair that had a lot to do with her efforts to inspire change as a feminist and leader."

***

It is clear from medical records, court records, police reports, and even a basic Google search that Tim had severe, lifelong mental and physical disabilities that clouded his perception and functionality. These mental and physical disabilities were the unique mix of his own set of genes, traumatic premature birth, and residuals from his medical treatments. No one was at fault for Tim's disabilities. Unfortunately, they were nuanced immovables in his experience of life, and there was little anyone could do to significantly improve his situation in the era he was born.

Today, the outlook for certain genetic disorders and prematurity is generally brighter compared to the 1960s. The study of endocrinology has also advanced substantially since Tim's childhood years of trial-and-error methodologies. So perhaps he would have had more resources today than were made available to him during his early years and his trajectory as he aged would have been different, but there also has to be room for the possibility that perhaps all the resources in the world would not have changed a thing for him.

Today, perhaps we cannot attribute as much systematic fault as we can retrospectively because in the 1960s, 1970s, and 1980s, the medical, mental health, and judicial systems were infused with considerably greater hierarchical values than they are today. As a part of the patient-consumer population, the general public is more empowered today than previous generations because we have unlimited access to a good portion of the same information doctors, therapists, and the court system do. Neither Susan nor Tim's generation had this benefit. Whatever the gods in the white coats, winged-back chairs, or behind the benches said, the general population had zero right to question. This power differential led to and enabled dependence on these systems—dependence that sometimes was completely blind. The general public didn't know what it didn't know, much in the same way the Catholic church, throughout the Middle Ages, discouraged laypeople from reading Bibles of their own. It's an age-old strategy of dictatorship—if we withhold the information, we control the interpretation and you peasant people can't ask questions, thereby giving us complete authority.

Luckily, the curtain has been pulled back on many Great Ozs of all fields since then, and today, we have the great privilege as a general population to seek out our own information on our human experience, ask questions, dialogue with experts, and provide informed consent. If we question a treatment plan proposed by a physician or mental health provider, we have access to alternatives. The "second opinion" option is implicitly available to us. Susan's generation did not have the privilege of choosing or rechoosing when questions, concerns, or doubts arose.

This principle of empowerment vs. dependence upon the system is especially important to note in this case because if we understand the system in which Susan was operating (insofar as we possibly can decades later), it is much easier to understand that the decisions she made for her only child were based on the cumulative knowledge she was dependent upon. In other words, Tim's care from the system wasn't authentically based on *her* decision, yet when the system's advice failed (and fostered Susan's murder), representatives of the system (i.e., doctors, lawyers, mental health providers) were quick to point the finger back at Susan's own personal judgment in saying, "Gee, what a monstrous mother!"

With so many experts in the mix of the Roman family, where was a single voice of reason in that dynamic? Why did no one advocate for Susan *and* for Tim long before it reached the point where adult mother and adult son were locked in a private prison of mutual resentment? With the files and files of "expert" notes on Susan and Tim Roman, one would think there would be documentation of at least one practical lifeline recommended to mitigate Tim's volcanic proclivities that only grew more volcanic as he aged. Long-term usage of steroids alone is associated with "uncontrollable outbursts of psychotic aggression, paranoia, and mood swings." Susan was not taking these drugs. Tim was, yet during his trial, everyone was just sure his murderous rage was due to Susan's outbursts, paranoia, nagging, and coddling.

When the subject and evidence of Tim's abuse of his mother were brought up in court, no one on the witness stand said, "God, I had no idea, or I would have stepped in." Everyone, whether in defense of Susan, Tim, or both had the same basic story: "Yes, we knew Tim was volatile and had frequent outbursts, but Susan started it, oh and also his thyroid levels were high, so he didn't mean it." Allegedly, this insane Hollywood mother was living in plain sight of everyone in Encino, and no one thought to call the proper authorities or somehow intervene on either account: Susan's alleged abuse or Tim's.

How would Susan have responded to an intervention on their toxic home life? Probably like the rest of us: badly—at first. No one likes their decisions and behaviors challenged, especially if those decisions and behaviors are in place to protect someone, but my question is, did anyone ever try? Truly try? I doubt it.

Of course, if someone noticed bruises on Susan's face or arms, she would have explained them away with "I ran into the door" or "I took a tumble off the bed," but the broader question is why the system itself did not provide resources ahead of the entrenchment of those patterns. Was Susan informed that Tim's medication cocktail could cause such extreme mental health side effects? If so, was she provided with a comprehensive treatment plan that gave Tim's medical team and psychologists all the same information so they could develop a unified treatment plan with checks and balances as he aged? I doubt it. Each expert threw his or her own specialty into the cauldron and hoped for the best—and the fragmented elixir brewed in that cauldron Susan and Tim both became dependent upon.

Susan and Tim were both victims of the broader system of "experts" in their lives, as well as their interpersonal ecosystem. They had bad counsel and a bunch of bystanders enabling this dance of codependency that eventually led to carnage. The universal truth at this point is twofold: 1. What type of interpersonal ecosystem are we in? Are we surrounded by bad counsel and a bunch of bystanders, or do we have good counsel and healthy accountability? 2. What kind of counsel and accountability are we providing for others in our own interpersonal ecosystems? If we begin to notice someone's boat spring a leak, do we turn our heads and think "well it's every man for himself out here," or do we lovingly offer a rope? One rope could have made the difference between life and death in Susan's case.

On March 13, 1964, twenty-eight-year-old Kitty Genovese was raped and stabbed to death outside her apartment building in Queens, New York. After her death, *The New York Times* reported the incident and claimed that more than thirty people witnessed the attack and did nothing to intervene. This case is what led to the psychological theory called "The Bystander Effect," which espouses that the more witnesses there are, the less likely it is that witnesses will intervene on a victim's behalf during a disturbing incident. In more recent years, the case of Kitty Genovese has been reexamined, and new interpretations of "The Bystander Effect" have been developed, but the original theory, whether related to Kitty Genovese or not, is still a real concept. Susan Cabot Roman was a victim of "The Bystander Effect" long before she became the victim of murder.

The Portrait of "Mother"

One of the first steps toward a more comprehensive view of a case study like Susan's is in acknowledging the presence of such a significant systematic bias in the sociopolitical era in which her life and death occurred. While Judge Darlene Schempp, who passed down Tim's charge and sentence, was in fact female, responders, attorneys, and most witnesses called were men—White men. In the 1980s, the sociological and judicial landscape of America was still dominated by sexism and racism at every turn.

Certainly, misogyny didn't just happen to pass over the case of Susan and Tim Roman. In piecing together the portrait of Susan posthumously, I believe to a certain degree that many of the men involved in the case (Michael Roman being no exception) filled in the blanks with their own sympathies for another White man in Timothy Scott Roman based on their own emotions, prejudices, and toxic masculinity. In short, Susan had a bunch of White men speaking for her, and that did nothing to help her side of the story. According to their interpretation, Tim had to either be a product of a failed system or a failed mother, and it was easier to point the finger at her and her alone.

To this point, Hayes et al. (2013) say, "[The] male lack of identification with women as victims may culminate in the form of victim-blaming due to a woman's behavior not fitting into traditional gender stereotypes of a 'good girl.'" It was no secret that Susan had a fiery personality with headstrong beliefs about her life and about Tim's. What others (primarily the male experts who teased out particulars after her death) interpreted as histrionic or vicious perhaps would not have been classified the same for a victim of the male persuasion.

While not directly related to the trial itself, a solid example of the same principle in Susan's career is in the great importance she placed on safety in her work. While filming John Barnwell's *Surrender — Hell!* in 1958, when the jungles of the Philippines became too much for Susan, she broke her contract and flew home as quickly as possible. Leaving mid-production perhaps isn't a great career-booster, but Susan was so protective of her own safety that she took the backlash in stride to do what she felt was best for her mental and physical health.

Before Paraluman's involvement in the film, Susan was virtually the only female in the cast except scant supports. Once she told Barnwell of her decision to leave, she was labeled a neurotic, over-the-top prude, but in considering her reality at the time (you know, leeches having to be burned off her skin with cigarettes), any number of individuals regardless of gender would probably be thrilled at the idea of going home too if they were not used to that type of unpredictability and danger in nature. In other words, the male perspective that was so pervasive in the sociopolitical environment of Susan's lifetime made for a narrow interpretation of her decisions both during and after her time on earth.

Actor Buddy Ebsen, most remembered as *The Beverly Hillbilly*'s "Uncle Jed," was originally cast as the Tin Man in MGM's technicolor masterpiece *The Wizard of Oz* in 1939. Several weeks into filming, after having recorded all of Tin Man's songs, he began to experience shortness of breath and body aches. He was hospitalized with these symptoms as they worsened, and his doctors determined Ebsen had aspirated much of the aluminum dust particles that made up his silver Tin Man makeup. His lungs had a nasty reaction to the substance, and he was forced to drop out of the production. Jack Haley replaced Ebsen, but the mid-production drop cost the studio a lot of time, money, and resources to mitigate Ebsen's decision—much more so than John Barnwell's production, yet no one shamed Ebsen or called him a petty neurotic because he did what was best for his mental and physical health at the time.

A respiratory reaction to aluminum dust might technically be worse than leeches, but there is a validity between the contrasts just the same. Before, during, and since *Surrender — Hell!* countless stars have dropped from productions mid-filming for far less concrete reasons than unhealthy working conditions, but Susan was part of a greater system that simply did not give women the benefit of the doubt during her life and in the aftermath of her death.

One of the reasons this biography of Susan's is so important is that at long last, a *female* feminist is displaying the fragments of her life's mosaic, and the pieces fall a little differently than the former "portrait of mother" that has for so long been hung in the hall of Hollywood history.

In the portrait painted of Susan during Tim's trials, the presence of misogyny leading the parade, so to speak, begs the question: would Susan have been judged as harshly had she not assumed both the mother and father roles in her parenthood? If there had been a consistent husband and father present in the Romans' lives at the time of Susan's death, would she still have been painted as a venomous villainess, or would the husband/father have (either overly or covertly) "protected" her legacy from such? Such presence also begs the question: if Susan had not been the beautiful siren of acclaim she was, would the case have been approached differently? If she were a single mother of average everything, would there have been such a parade at all?

Tim's litany of developmental challenges weren't anyone's fault. Given the comorbidity of Tim's genetic disorders and the residuals of his traumatic birth, his innate challenges were no one's doing. The treatment prescribed by his medical specialists, including steroids, testosterone, and the human growth hormone injections were, at the time, medically sound treatments, but surely had effects on his range of functionality from emotional regulation to tendencies of physical aggression.

Ok, Mother Teresa, she wasn't, but my informed opinion of Susan after months of researching her character is that she was first human, then mother. Susan considered her motherhood the most significant role in her life, her greatest priority, and her greatest joy. That's one of the dynamics that makes this story so incredibly sad. If Susan had approached her motherhood apathetically and constantly left Tim with strangers, didn't come home for days or weeks at a time, provided nothing in the way of basic necessities, and generally left him to fend for himself the way her parent figures in foster care had done to her, the portrait of her motherhood would have been altogether different. There may be some who argue he would have been better off if that *had* been the case, and who knows? But the fact that Susan cared so very deeply for Tim that she over-mothered is perhaps the core sticking-point of this tragedy.

Science Experiments

When medical experts first developed the human growth hormone in the 1950s, it wasn't some mad scientist in the basement kind of deal; it was a grand discovery that brought hope to millions suffering from conditions similar to Tim's dwarfism. When the experiments began in the late 1950s, in which thousands of children were given injections to boost their growth, many parents were ecstatic to have such innovation available to them, however experimental it was considered. Susan was one of those millions who jumped at the chance to give her child a better quality of life promised by the medical professionals. It wasn't until after the enzyme contamination was discovered in the 1980s that the experiments were viewed as creepy Area 51 stuff.

The press's comparison of Susan's on-screen portrayal of "Janice Starlin" in *The Wasp Woman* and Tim's involvement in the experimental stuff decades before is partly why the series of studies were eventually categorized with MKUltra and UFOs. No one knew until years after the studies were conducted that the cadaver enzymes had contaminated the bloodstreams and brain tissue of nearly all study participants across the globe. Scientists supposedly used a thorough purification process after extracting the enzymes from cadavers, but the CJD prion wasn't something readily detected, nor something anyone was looking for, so its particles passed through the purification process unfazed.

Unfortunately, several people had to die before the experts involved knew there was even an issue. It took some thorough investigation to determine the cause of the CJD diagnoses that led to the deaths and the correlation between the injections decades earlier and the disease. When the evidence became too solid to ignore, the medical groups involved in the experiments had no choice but to admit unintentional fault. Hundreds of lawsuits were filed all over the globe for the anguish parents and their children went through upon learning they may or may not meet with a sudden and brutal fatal end.

It is plausible that Susan's physical and mental deterioration began to speed up subsequent to Tim's doctors revealing the awful news to her of contamination. After a lifetime of always being under someone else's ownership with bad counsel and a bunch of bystanders for support, the news of Tim's potential for CJD was simply too much for her. A thick resignation took over.

I truly believe Susan and the thousands of other parents who permitted their children to participate in the human growth hormone study were doing the next right thing for their child and/or children according to what the professionals of the 1950s-1980s recommended. Some experiments turn out wonderful, life-saving results, while others turn out horrible, brain-killing ones. No other parents were painted (at least not publicly) as deranged sadists because they signed the waiver for their child and/or children to be experimentally treated, yet Susan was because of a little B-movie from 1959.

The parallels between *The Wasp Woman* and Tim's injections are really ironic, I'll admit, but the media and Tim's defense attorneys went too far. They drew upon this passing irony and brought it center stage to make the case of Susan as a lunatic. In close review of the facts of this case beyond the yellow journalism, I am convinced that Susan made the best decision for Tim she could at the time, given the level of information she had when she signed that waiver—just as the hundreds and thousands of other parents did within the context of the same study. Because Susan was in a bug-lady sci-fi film doesn't mean she had mad scientist or delusional ideals about such a study, it means she made the best decision for Tim that she could at the time, and unfortunately that decision turned out to have fatal consequences. After learning of the serum's contamination, the self-shame of that decision (however informed it was at the time) ate her alive, and she didn't have the resourcing to ever come back up.

Resourcing

From the beginning of Susan's story to the ghastly end, one of the most obvious elements missing for her was resourcing. During her tumultuous childhood beginning in Boston, she had the misfortune of growing up in the rudimentary stages of foster care, in part, because no one knew the complexities of the postpartum depression from which her mother, Muriel, suffered.

The foster care system is still imperfect, as nearly all systems are, but in the 1930s and 1940s, it was a ramshackled "good idea" that hadn't yet found its settlement, much to the detriment of many millions of children like Susan. The families that Susan was shuffled in and out of left hosts of permanent scars on her psyche, and in her journey toward healing, she was met with inadequate mental health resources from the 1940s to the 1980s that may have actually done more harm than good.

It's easy to get caught up in the fencing of blame or "if onlys," but there's a solid call to action within the gross lack of resourcing throughout each of Susan's life stages. While we could blame the historical era itself, we must realize our own susceptibility to apathy on social justice issues that could result in the eventual backsliding of the resourcing our world has worked toward since Susan's generation.

Quality community resourcing for any of the following issues could have made a difference in the story of Susan Cabot Roman and Timothy Scott Roman: postpartum depression, foster care, domestic violence, sexual, physical, and emotional abuse, depression, anxiety, PTSD, child-to-parent domestic violence, bullying, codependency, and suicidal ideation. These social issues were just as important during Susan's lifetime as they are today, but informed awareness was virtually nonexistent then. While we are fortunate in the 2020s to have a more enlightened perspective from which to consider these issues compared to Susan's era, awareness is only part of the equation. We still have a long way to go to make sure that the story of Susan Cabot Roman doesn't repeat. Advocacy for others and advocacy for self is key to not only improving our personal ecosystems, but our world. No one advocated for the Roman family when they were unable to advocate for themselves.

Not only was Susan's murder utterly heinous, senseless, and uncalled for, but it was also completely preventable. My belief is that if the entire Roman family had had the support they needed, Timothy Scott Roman would not have had such an opportunity to continue in his pattern of domestic violence toward his mother that ultimately resulted in her brutal murder. I do not blame Susan for not blowing the whistle on Tim's violence toward her; I blame the professionals he regularly consulted with who knew of his volcanic tendencies, yet still blamed Susan once those tendencies reached their climax.

The bad counsel and a bunch of bystanders failed Susan and Tim both. In my study of Susan's life, she gave Tim every possible resource she could to help him learn the psychoeducational skills he needed to manage his emotions and cope with life. She enrolled him in public school to help him acclimate to society norms, and she enrolled him in martial arts training to help him learn self-control and self-defense. For his entire life, she attempted to enrich him through art, music, science, and social graces, but he was incapable of applying those skills. That incapability is no one's fault, but to blame his mother for how that incapability later manifested in his pattern of abuse is unconscionable.

Would Tim's trial have been handled differently today than it was in the 1980s? I would like to think yes, but I really don't know. Even on the far side of the third wave of feminism and movements like #MeToo, society is still replete with victim-blaming and mother-blaming, especially in institutional contexts, which is something that cases like Susan's remind us as a society to be mindful of on both small and large scales.

Song of the Heart

It's inconceivable to think the boy whose birth nearly killed Susan - the boy she sang to through the oxygen tent in that Washington D.C. hospital for four months—the boy she loved and protected through more than twenty years of medical, social, and development difficulties—the boy she walked to class to help him avoid bullies—the boy she provided for and prayed for—the boy she nearly worshipped could grow into a man so full of rage, resentment, and disdain for her that he could come to her in the dead of night while she slept and bludgeon her brains out with a barbell.

Acclaimed actor, director, and producer Elliott Lewis wrote many beautiful radio plays for the anthology *Suspense*. One play he wrote in 1948 is called "Song of the Heart," and the folklore within the script, I believe, speaks to Susan's great love for Tim that while she was being abused by him in the years leading up to her death, she was still concerned with his well-being."

> *That record tells a story about a boy and his mother. The boy lived at home with his mother, and the boy met a girl. And the mother didn't like the girl and warned the boy away from her. But the girl used all her wiles on the boy and the boy turned against his mother. And the girl told him that proof of his love for her would be that he killed his mother. And proof of the killing would be that he brought the girl his mother's heart. And so the poor boy killed his mother and took her heart to bring it to the girl. And on the way, he stumbled and fell, and the heart escaped his hands. And before he could get to his feet again or even see if he was injured from the fall, the heart spoke and the heart said to him, 'Are you hurt, my son?'*

There is no valid defense for Tim's actions on the night of December 10, 1986. There is, however, redemption in a more accurate portrait of Susan Cabot Roman compared to the one painted during the course of Tim's trials.

The Portrait of Redemption

In my opinion, there was little vindication for Susan during or after Tim's trials despite the several people who testified on her behalf. Similarly, if you're a "the punishment should fit the crime" kind of person, there was little vindication in Tim's sentencing. Perhaps through the thick of the gruesome details, police reports, and testimonies of expert witnesses, we can only, nearly forty years later, claim some personal vindication for Susan by holding on to the tiny glimmers of redemption sprinkled throughout her story—and now the more balanced, comprehensive interpretation of such. Humanity can never truly reach vindication in cases of such savagery as matricide, because even if Tim had been immediately sentenced to the electric chair after his initial confession, still where would the vindication for Susan be?

So, in place of vindication, may I suggest instead a more realistic concept: redemption. Redemption can always be fostered through the examination of alternative perspectives of one-dimensional victim-blaming narratives. And the understanding of redemption I personally recommend for this case can be found within the repainting of Susan's portrait.

I have tried, through this book, to carefully sand off the inaccurate layers of oil paint so sloppily painted over the self-portrait Susan inadvertently painted through the legacy of her life. The two main colors used by the misogynistically framed court proceedings and media circus were the thick matte swamp green of victim-blaming and the glossy candy apple red of mother-blaming.

Luckily, the green and red layers of spin were simply acrylic, so the lovely oil painting on the canvas beneath has gone largely untouched. Metaphorically, the oils Susan used to paint her own legacy were causative oils, which harden on canvas into an impenetrable state. Allow me to describe the painting I see now that the layers are removed.

I see a realistic painting of traditional technique. The painting is of a beautiful woman of intensity with black hair, brown eyes, and olive skin. It is a multidimensional painting with sharp hues of hinted depth and shaded angles of both darkness and light. It is a vibrant and haunting portrait that captures the centered, head-and-shoulders view of Harriet Shapiro—Susan Cabot Roman.

I see brushstrokes of black signifying a lifetime of chambered hurts that began in her early childhood and ended in the home-prison she was in with Tim. The black signifies the brutal cogs of foster care after her mother was taken away. The black signifies the physical, sexual, and emotional abuse she suffered in the homes of strangers she was forced to call her "family." The black signifies the currents of pain, betrayal, loss, and defeat that ran through her earthly years of heartbreak, rejection, and almost constant fight-or-flight survival. The gradient of the black strokes only gets blacker as they trail toward the frame's edge, signifying the despair of Susan's final days, climaxing in the blackest of all on December 10, 1986.

I see dotted brushstrokes of ivory edged in emerald green, signifying the early jazzy days of Greenwich Village where Harriet Shapiro Sacker turned to Susan Cabot and found her artistic voice at The Village Barn. In certain places, the gradient of ivory swirls with the emerald green, signifying the hope of La Scala and then of Hollywood stardom as Susan began her ascent to the silver screen with Martin Sacker by her side.

I see thick brushstrokes of light pink edged in champagne gold signifying the rich, playful days of Old Hollywood when a beautiful, young Susan Cabot was in her prime—when she was dressed in furs and Van Cleef & Arpels laughing and dancing in swank nightspots on Sunset Blvd. with Hollywood's smoky Golden Age crowds—then later the rich, playful days of Broadway rehearsals in New York City, Ritz Carlton dinners, and limousine rides with tuxedoed dignitaries.

I see swirling brushstrokes of sky blue signifying the sweet early days of Tim's childhood when Susan was just beginning to confidently assume her role as mother, excited about what bright, promising future she envisioned for her son. The sky blue billows around the canvas as a focal point of the painting—such promise and tenderness radiate from the pigmentation.

I see bold brushstrokes of burnt orange signifying the feministic fury Susan held in strongarming the countless traumas of her lifetime. The burnt orange is crisp and bright in signifying the resiliency of her personhood and self-agency, as she independently raised her son while pursuing her career in the face of such misogynistic impediment.

I see deliberate brushstrokes of deep, blood red for the primal love she felt for her only child, Timothy Scott Roman, who she almost died giving birth to and who she did die giving life to.

So, with that painting, the defense of Susan Cabot Roman rests.

For support, resources, and advice for your safety, call the National Domestic Violence Hotline.

1-800-799-SAFE (7233)

Appendix
Selected Screen Performances of Susan Cabot

Kiss of Death (1947)

Henry Hathaway's *Kiss of Death* is a crime film starring Victor Mature, Brian Donlevy, and Richard Widmark (in his film debut). *Kiss of Death* tells the story of former criminal "Nick Bianco" who becomes an informant for the police to protect his family. The film received critical acclaim for its gripping storyline and standout performances, particularly from Richard Widmark, who received an Academy Award nomination for Best Supporting Actor. *Kiss of Death* is considered a classic film noir and remains a significant contribution to the genre. This was Susan's first film role; she plays the role of "restaurant patron."

On the Isle of Samoa (1950)

William Berke's *On the Isle of Samoa* tells the story of former airman "Kenneth Crandall" (played by Jon Hall) who steals an airplane after a botched robbery, but crashes on the uncharted island of Tongaluha. There he is befriended by the island's "Chief Tihoti," the beautiful native girl, "Moana," and the island's only other White man, "Peter Appleton." Crandall repairs the plane and builds an airstrip to return to civilization, leaving the lovestruck Moana behind. Susan plays the role of island native "Moana."

The Enforcer (1951)

Bretaigne Windust and Raoul Walsh's *The Enforcer* is a crime drama starring Humphrey Bogart as "District Attorney Martin Ferguson" and Zero

Mostel as "Joseph Rico," a notorious gangster. The story revolves around Ferguson's efforts to bring Rico to justice for his involvement in organized crime. Susan portrays the role of "Nina Lombardo" in the film.

Tomahawk (1951)

George Sherman's Western film *Tomahawk*, starring Van Heflin, Yvonne De Carlo, and Alex Nicol, is the story of a frontier scout in his attempts to mend relations between the Sioux Indians and the United States Army. The film received positive reviews for its realistic portrayal of the time period and its engaging storyline. Susan portrays the beautiful "Monahseetah."

The Prince Who Was a Thief (1951)

Rudolph Maté's *The Prince Who Was a Thief* is based on writer Theodore Dreiser's short story of thirteenth-century Tangiers, in which assassin "Yussef" (played by Everett Sloane) is commissioned to kill young Prince Hussein. Yussef finds he cannot complete the mission and keeps "Julna" (played by Tony Curtis) to raise as his own. Unaware of his imperial blood, Julna grows up to become a thief like the man who raised him. Susan portrays a small, uncredited role in the film.

Flame of Araby (1951)

Charles Lamont's *Flame of Araby* tells of the lovely Arabian Princess Tanya (played by Maureen O'Hara) who feuds with Bedouin chief "Tamerlane" (played by Jeff Chandler) over ownership of a prized stallion. They quickly put their differences aside, however, to unite in opposition to their mutual enemies: the Corsair Lords. Susan portrays the role of palace dancer "Clio."

The Battle at Apache Pass (1952)

George Sherman's Western *The Battle at Apache Pass*, starring John Lund, follows the tribes of Cochise (played by Jeff Chandler) and Geronimo (played by Jay Silverheels) in their complex frontier relations with the United States Army. Susan portrays "Nona," the wife of Chief Cochise.

The Duel at Silver Creek (1952)

In Don Siegel's first Western film, *The Duel at Silver Creek,* Audie Murphy stars as a young gunslinger seeking revenge for his father's murder. Tomboy "Jane 'Dusty' Fargo" (played by Susan Cabot) joins the Silver Kid in his pursuit of the murderous claim jumpers and ends up falling for the brave avenger.

Son of Ali Baba (1952)

In Kurt Neumann's romantic-adventure film *Son of Ali Baba* (1952), Tony Curtis portrays "Kashma Baba," the son of infamous Arabian hero "Ali Baba," with Piper Laurie as "Princess Azura of Fez, Kiki," his central love interest. "Kashma" is a dedicated Persian military cadet, but a perennial playboy in his personal life. The film tells the story of "Kashma's" brushes with love and rivalry within the shadow cast by his father's legacy. Susan portrays supporting character "Tala," one of the many Arabian beauties enamored with "Kashma."

Gunsmoke (1953)

Nathan Juran's 1953 *Gunsmoke* stars Audie Murphy as "Reb Kittridge," a hired gun sent to obtain deeds from ranchers who have refused to sell out to the land-hungry "Matt Telford" (played by Donald Randolph). During his mission, Reb falls in love with "Rita Saxon," the daughter of one of the ranchers from whom he was sent to claim a deed. Susan portrays the role of "Rita Saxon."

Ride Clear of Diablo (1954)

Jesse Hibbs' *Ride Clear of Diablo* is another classic Western tale. Audie Murphy portrays railroad man "Clay O'Mara" in his plight to destroy those responsible for his father's murder. Susan portrays "Laurie Kenyon," O'Mara's love interest, who aids him on his journey toward vindication.

Kraft Theatre (1957)

Season 10, Episode 42 "The First and the Last"

Carnival Rock (1957)

Roger Corman's *Carnival Rock* is the rockabilly story of carnival pier nightclub owner "Christy" (played by David J. Stewart) who romantically pursues starlet "Natalie Cook" (played by Susan Cabot) to the point of sheer madness. Susan's character has musical numbers in the film, along with pop music stars of the 1950s, including The Platters, David Houston, Bob Luman and His Shadows, and The Blockbusters.

Sorority Girl (1957)

Roger Corman's *Sorority Girl* tells the sordid story of neurotic college student, "Sabra Tanner" (played by Susan Cabot), who systematically destroys relations with her peers on her college campus. Spoiled, willful, and conniving, "Sabra" increasingly resorts to violence and blackmail in maladaptively striving for love and affection until the film's grim conclusion.

The Saga of the Viking Women and Their Voyage to the Waters of the Great Sea Serpent (1957)

Roger Corman's *The Saga of the Viking Women and Their Voyage to the Waters of the Great Sea Serpent* (1957) is an adventure film that follows the seafaring journey of a group of Viking women in the search for their missing Viking men. During their harrowing journey, they encounter a sea serpent that destroys their ship, leaving them stranded in a foreign land where they are taken captive. Susan portrays fiery Viking woman, "Enger."

Fort Massacre (1958)

Joseph Newman's *Fort Massacre* follows a group of Union soldiers led by "Sergeant Vinson" (played by Joel McCrea) as they are ambushed by Apache warriors while on a mission to deliver a peace treaty. Like many

Westerns, the film explores themes of survival, loyalty, and the harsh realities of war. Susan portrays the role of "Piute Girl."

War of the Satellites (1958)

Roger Corman's *War of the Satellites*, starring Dick Miller and Susan Cabot, is the story of an invisible entity that wages war against planet Earth when the United Nations fails to heed warnings during attempts to assemble the first space satellite. Susan portrays the role of the lead female scientist, "Sybil Carrington," opposite Dick Miller.

Machine-Gun Kelly (1958)

Roger Corman's pseudo-biographical film *Machine-Gun Kelly* delves into the life and career of notorious Prohibition gangster George "Machine-Gun" Kelly, played by Charles Bronson. Susan portrays Kelly's partner-in-crime turned love interest, "Flo Becker."

Have Gun — Will Travel (1958)
Season 1 Episode 19 "The High Graders"

Have Gun — Will Travel was Andrew V. McLaglen's Western television series starring Richard Boone as the heroic "Paladin." "The High Graders" episode follows Paladin in his attempts to solve the mystery of his tailor's death. Susan portrays the role of supporting character "Angela."

Have Gun — Will Travel (1959)
Season 2 Episode 34 "Comanche"

Have Gun — Will Travel, Andrew V. McLaglen's Western television series starring Richard Boone as the heroic "Paladin." The "Comanche" episode follows Paladin in his adventures to Indian territory in search of a United States Army corporal gone missing. Susan portrays the supporting role of "Becky Gray Carver."

The Wasp Woman (1959)

Roger Corman's cult classic *Wasp Woman* is the sci-fi story of cosmetics corporation president "Janice Starlin," (played by Susan Cabot) who experiments with a youth serum developed from the extract of wasps. The serum is successful in restoring Janice's youth, but it comes with deadly side effects.

Surrender — Hell! (1959)

John Barnwell's *Surrender — Hell!* is a war drama based on the memoir of WWII commander, Lt. Donald D. Blackburn, in his refusal to surrender to the Japanese or the treacherous conditions of the island of Luzon. Blackburn (played by Keith Andes) leads a group of natives in a fight against the Japanese invasion. Susan portrays the role of "Delia Guerrero" who helps Blackburn survive.

Bracken's World (1970)
Season 1 Episode 26 "One, Two, Three…Cry"

Set in the behind-the-scenes dramas of "Century Studios," "John Bracken" (played by Warren Stevens) is the studio's god-like CEO. In the episode "One, Two, Three…Cry," Paulette hires an acting coach to improve her chances of getting acting jobs with the studio. This acting coach she hires, however, is notorious for his dubious intentions with young starlets. Susan portrays the supporting role of "Henrietta."

Bibliography

Adams, M. "Manager Dreamed Up Name: Boston-Born Susan Cabot No Kin to Lodge or Lowell." *Boston Globe*, September 18, 1959.

Bieler, Z. "Varied Roles Have Marked Career of Hollywood Actress." *Montreal Star*, May 22, 1959.

Bolton, W. "Looking Sideways." *Buffalo News*, March 28, 1956.

Holt, Marilyn Irvin. *The Orphan Trains: Placing Out in America*. Lincoln: Bison Books, 1994.

Hopper, Hedda. "Jeffery Lynn Will Star in 'Forty Notches.'" *Los Angeles Times*, December 2, 1950.

Johnson, E. "On the Record." *Daily News*, May 23, 1951.

Knox, Paul. "Dorchester, Boston." In *Palimpsests: Biographies of 50 City Districts—International Case Studies of Urban Change*, 64–69. Basel: Birkhäuser, 2012. https://doi.org/10.1515/9783034612128.64.

Lane, L. "Beware Fatigue Signals, Warns Star Susan Cabot." *Ottawa Citizen*, March 22, 1952.

Laron, Z. "The Era of Cadaveric Pituitary–Extracted Human Growth Hormone (1958–1985): Biological and Clinical Aspects." *Pediatric Endocrinology Reviews* 16, suppl. 1 (2018): 11–16. https://doi.org/10.17458/per.vol16.2018.la.hghcadavericpituitary. PMID: 30378778.

Mabbott, L. "Rising Young Actress Prefers 'Bad Girl Rolls' [sic]." *Rapid City Journal*, June 11, 1950.

Manners, D. *Philadelphia Inquirer*, June 10, 1966.

McCarthy, E., and B. M. Murphy, eds. *Lost Souls of Horror and the Gothic: Fifty-Four Neglected Authors, Actors, Artists, and Others*. Jefferson, NC: McFarland & Company, 2016.

n.a. "The Second Feature." *Buffalo News*, July 27, 1950.

—"Training for an Apache Housewife." *Redondo Reflex*, February 29, 1952.

—"Susan Cabot Debuts in Laguna Play Tomorrow." *Los Angeles Evening Citizen News*, August 18, 1952.

—"Pint-Sized Actresses Find Hollywood 'Cold.'" *Long Beach Press-Telegram*, October 12, 1953.

—"Half-Pint Susan Plugs for More Murphy Movies." *Valley Times*, November 12, 1953.

—"To Open in Myrtle Beach: Actress Susan Cabot Hopes for Happy Home and Family." *Charlotte Observer*, June 30, 1956.

—"Ex-Star Susan Cabot Killed; Son Arrested." *Buffalo News*, December 12, 1986.

—"Actress' Son Denies He Is Her Murderer." *Desert Dispatch*, June 10, 1987.

Plunz, Richard, and Kenneth T. Jackson. *A History of Housing in New York City*. Rev. ed. New York: Columbia University Press, 2016. https://doi.org/10.7312/plun17834.

Rawson, Michael. *Eden on the Charles: The Making of Boston*. Cambridge, MA: Harvard University Press, 2010. https://doi.org/10.4159/9780674058552.

Royal, D. "Meet... Susan Cabot." *Paducah Sun*, May 29, 1959.

Wagner, Laura. *Hollywood's Hard-Luck Ladies*. Jefferson, NC: McFarland & Company, 2020.

Wilson, E. "Crazy Things Happen to Susan." *News and Observer*, September 13, 1959.

HISTRIA BOOKS

HISTRIA A&E

Fine Books from the world of Arts and Entertainment

For these and other great books visit

HistriaBooks.com